Attlee's Labour Governments
1945–51

IN THE SAME SERIES

General Editors: Eric J. Evans and P.D. King

LANCASTER PAMPHLETS

Attlee's Labour Governments 1945–51

Robert Pearce

London and New York

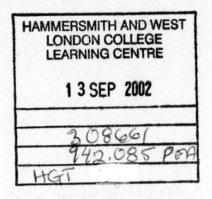
First published 1994
by Routledge
11 New Fetter Lane, London EC4P 4EE

Simultaneously published in the USA and Canada
by Routledge
29 West 35th Street, New York, NY 10001

© *1994 Robert Pearce*

Typeset in Bembo by
Ponting–Green Publishing Services, Chesham, Bucks
Printed in Great Britain by
Clays Ltd, St Ives plc

British Library Cataloguing in Publication Data
A catalogue record for this book is available from the British Library

Library of Congress Cataloging in Publication Data
Pearce, R.D. (Robert D.)
Attlee's labour governments 1945–51/Robert Pearce.
p. cm. – (Lancaster pamphlets)
Includes bibliographical references
1. Attlee, C.R. (Clement Richard), 1883–1967.
2. Great Britain–Politics and government–1945–1964
3. Labour party (Great Britain)
I. Title. II. Series.
DA588.P43 1994
324.24107–dc20 93–15764

ISBN 0–415–08893–3

Contents

Foreword

Lancaster Pamphlets offer concise and up-to-date accounts of major historical topics, primarily for the help of students preparing for Advanced Level examinations, though they should also be of value to those pursuing introductory courses in universities and other institutions of higher education. Without being all-embracing, their aims are to bring some of the central themes or problems confronting students and teachers into sharper focus than the textbook writer can hope to do; to provide the reader with some of the results of recent research which the textbook may not embody; and to stimulate thought about the whole interpretation of the topic under discussion.

Chronology

1945

8 May	VE (Victory in Europe) Day.
4 June	Churchill's 'Gestapo' broadcast.
5 July	General election. Results announced on 26 July. Labour won 393 seats, Conservatives 213.
6 August	Atomic bomb dropped on Hiroshima. Nagasaki bombed three days later.
14 August	Keynes warned politicians of a 'financial Dunkirk'.
15 August	Japan surrendered unconditionally.
21 August	Truman abruptly ended Lend-Lease.
14 October	Troops called in to unload food during dock strike.
6 December	US loan agreement signed in Washington; accepted by the House of Commons later in the month.

1946

1 March	Bank of England nationalised.
22 May	Trade Disputes Act repealed.
30 May	Bread rationing began.
22 July	King David Hotel blown up in Jerusalem.
1 August	National Insurance Act received royal assent.

1947

1 January	Nationalisation of coal and of Cable and Wireless.
8 January	Attlee and other ministers authorised the manufacture of a British atomic bomb.
24 January	Severe weather hit Britain, causing economic crisis.
14 February	Palestine issue referred by Britain to the UN.
20 February	Mountbatten appointed Viceroy of India. Power to be transferred not later than June 1948.
15 March	Worst floods recorded in England.
1 April	School-leaving age raised to 15.
3 June	Power to be transferred in India on 15 August 1947.
5 June	George Marshall's speech on aid to Europe.
15 July	Sterling made convertible into dollars.
15 August	India and Pakistan became independent.
21 August	Sterling convertibility suspended.
29 September	Cripps became Minister of Economic Affairs.
8 November	Potato rationing introduced.
13 November	Dalton resigned; Cripps became Chancellor of the Exchequer.

1948

1 January	Nationalisation of the railways.
4 January	Independence of Burma.
10 February	Independence of Ceylon.
27 February	Communist coup in Czechoslovakia.
1 April	Nationalisation of electricity.
14 May	End of the mandate in Palestine.
26 May	Berlin airlift began.
28 June	State of Emergency declared as dockers began unofficial strike.
5 July	National Health Service inaugurated.
25 July	Bread rationing ended.
5 November	Wilson's 'bonfire of controls'.

1949

15 March	Clothes rationing ended.
4 April	North Atlantic Treaty Organisation agreement signed in Washington.
24 April	Chocolate and sweet rationing ended.

27 April	The 'London Declaration' on the nature of the Commonwealth: the King was Head of the Commonwealth, and thus republican status was compatible with Commonwealth membership.
1 May	Nationalisation of gas industry.
12 May	End of Berlin blockade.
1 July	Three-week dock strike began in London. Troops were used to move food.
18 September	Devaluation of sterling from $4.03 to $2.80.
26 October	Britain recognised Mao's People's Republic of China.
24 November	Nationalisation of iron and steel to become effective after another general election.
16 December	Parliament Bill received royal assent.

1950

23 February	General election: Labour won an overall majority of five seats.
19 April	Two-week London dock strike. Troops used.
25 June	Cabinet rejected the Schuman Plan for a European Coal and Steel Community. North Korean troops invaded South Korea.
2 September	TUC voted against continuing the wage freeze.
15 September	National service extended from eighteen months to two years.
19 October	Gaitskell replaced Cripps as Chancellor.

1951

17 January	Aneurin Bevan became Minister of Labour.
28 January	Reduction of the meat ration.
15 February	Iron and steel nationalisation.
9 March	Morrison succeeded Ernest Bevin as Foreign Secretary.
15 March	Iran nationalised Anglo-Iranian Oil Company.
14 April	Death of Ernest Bevin.
21 April	Resignation of Bevan over health service charges.
22 April	Resignation of Wilson.
3 May	Festival of Britain opened.
25 October	General Election. Labour won most votes but Conservatives gained overall majority of seventeen.

1
Introduction

'All our enemies having surrendered unconditionally, or being about to do so,' wrote former wartime Prime Minister Winston Churchill, 'I was instantly dismissed by the British electorate.' He was not the only one to be shocked by the results of the 1945 general election. Political commentators were equally amazed. Almost everyone, including Labour's leaders, had predicted a comfortable Conservative victory. Yet, in retrospect, it is hard to understand such views. Labour's victory now seems 'over-determined', in that there are more than enough plausible explanations to account for it.

Periods of warfare – that is to say of violence, brutality and general mayhem – are often followed by outbreaks of tender idealism whose most common symptom is the vision of a fairer society. As in 1918, with 'a fit country for heroes to live in', so in 1945, when the Labour party was closely associated with hopes for better housing and a welfare state. In consequence the election result no longer seems even mildly surprising. Indeed it has been said that, by the time of the campaign, Labour did not have to win the election but merely avoid losing it. Perhaps the only puzzle, given recent historical accounts, is that Attlee's Labour party, while admittedly achieving a great victory with 61 per cent of seats and an overall majority of 146, won only 47.8 per cent of total votes cast.

However, if one area of controversy has subsided, at least

temporarily, others show no signs of generating other than heated disagreement. First, there is the issue of personnel. In particular, what are we to make of the Prime Minister, Clement Attlee? Was he, as Churchill joked, merely a 'sheep in sheep's clothing', 'a modest man with plenty to be modest about'? Historians have described him as smaller, not larger, than life, 'underwhelming' rather than overwhelming. But how could such an extraordinarily ordinary man have led the Labour party for twenty years and stayed at the top of the greasy pole for six? Or was he in fact a highly efficient executive and superb chairman of committee, with an excellent understanding of his party and grasp of the government machine, one of the very best prime ministers in modern history? Both Attlees have found their places in recent historiography. Into the impenetrable silences of this essentially shy man – dubbed by George VI 'Clam', rather than Clem, Attlee, a man so self-effacing that he sometimes disappeared altogether – have been read both inadequacy and delphic understanding. Attlee's ability to parry reporters' queries and avoid self-revelation has seemed to some historians to betray a determination to preserve some personal mystery. Was Attlee the proverbial sphinx, guarding its secret, or (as Bismarck said of Louis Napoleon) a 'sphinx without a riddle'?

More fundamentally, what place should be assigned to Attlee's governments in British history? Were the years 1945–51 a period of bold legislative achievement which changed Britain permanently – though whether for good or ill is another area of contention – and established a consensus in British politics that lasted until the Thatcher years, in the 1980s? Or, on the contrary, was this period one of wretched anticlimax, a dénouement after the truly revolutionary years of the 'people's war'? According to this latter view, the consensus between the major parties had been forged before the 1945 election, so that all Labour had to do afterwards was follow the instructions on wartime blueprints. It has been argued that the Conservatives would have done no less, especially given the conversion of sections of the Whitehall establishment to the new gospel, stressing welfare and a managed economy, according to Keynes and Beveridge.

In view of this controversy, it is not surprising that almost every possible political label has been assigned to the Labour governments, from revolutionary to reactionary. Attlee is said by some to have brought about a socialist revolution, or at any rate to have taken Britain a good way along the road to socialism; but others insist that he merely reinvigorated the old capitalist system by limited doses of welfare and public ownership. Much of course depends on how 'socialism' is defined, an issue not helped by the fact that no one knows how to define it. Many writers, like Peter Clarke, insist that 'socialism' has no meaning except as the antithesis of 'capitalism', that is to say as the common rather than the private ownership of the means of production. The only problem with such clarity is that many self-styled socialists, concerned more with moral ends than economic means, define it very differently. To them it means a more equal and more caring society. Herbert Morrison, perhaps affecting cynicism, once remarked that socialism 'is what Labour governments do'; but the real cynics aver that socialism is merely what Labour spokesmen or Tory scaremongers say they will do. Recent writers like Kenneth Morgan and Peter Hennessy have cut through the Gordian knot by interpreting 1945–51 not in ideological terms at all but in less problematic terms of efficiency and effectiveness. Although pointing to Labour's failings and shortcomings, they nevertheless praise Attlee's administrations highly. But while they highlight Labour's successes, other historians point to the governments' failures, insisting that they were dominated by circumstances and did not leave a genuine impress on British history.

This uncertainty is not a consequence of any shortage of information. We know a vast amount about 1945–51: official papers were released some years ago, and they have been supplemented by the diaries of several cabinet ministers. Biographers have also been constructively at work, producing one-, two- and even three-volume works on such key figures as Attlee, Bevin, Morrison, Bevan, Dalton and Gaitskell. Important economic histories have also been written. We are in fact unlikely to learn much more about what happened in this period. But highly contrasting judgements and interpretations continue to be provided.

No doubt such variety stems in part from the nature of historical study: there is, and can be, no finality in history. And yet it is hard to avoid the conclusion that other forces are important as well. One is political bias. The postwar world is

3

generally seen as 'contemporary history' and still arouses political passions and prejudices. The period 1945–51 has been used by Labour supporters to vaunt what a Labour government can do and by Tory supporters to warn against what a Labour government would do if the electorate were unwise enough to return another. Furthermore, our perspective on the immediate postwar period depends very much on present and future events, including issues like East-West relations, the nationalisation or privatisation of industry and the funding of the National Health Service. Indeed, only the future will decide whether the initiatives of the Labour governments constituted fruitful growths or dead ends.

Students must be on their guard against the mythology that has grown up about 1945–51 and against political bias, including their own. One way of minimising bias is by an awareness of the criteria by which judgements are made. Everyone makes judgements; it is impossible not to do so. But conflicting verdicts can be better understood if we are conscious of the yardsticks used by those who formulate them. Some critics, especially on the left of the political spectrum, measure the achievements of the governments against theoretical socialist models: most often they condemn Attlee and the other ministers for not doing what they should have done. Sometimes they even blame them for engaging in bourgeois parliamentary democracy at all! Even right-wing critics reproach the governments for having the wrong aims and, inevitably, the wrong means for achieving them. Others compare the achievements of the governments with their aims, especially those set before the electorate in their 1945 manifesto; with what they suppose a Tory government in the same situation would have done (inevitably a fairly speculative business); or with what various other British governments have achieved. Many historians try to see these years from the perspectives of the politicians themselves, viewing their work along with the day-to-day circumstances and problems which limited political freedom of action. What from one perspective may seem a 'failure' – like the governments' housing record – may from another be judged a 'success', after due recognition of intractable conditions. Some historians give prominence to one area of political activity, for instance seeing foreign policy as the touchstone of their work, others to vastly different ones.

How much importance should historians assign to the implementation of family allowances as against the independence of India, or the raising of the school-leaving age against the formation of NATO? How can we weigh in the balance the nationalisation of coal and the provision of false teeth? The governments' work was indeed multifarious, and we should be careful not to allow our particular concern with one area to colour our overall verdict unduly. Perhaps no single general verdict will be possible. The instinct to 'label' à la *1066 and All That* is sometimes hard to resist – but it is not always 'a good thing'! Indeed, quite often such labels can be a substitute for genuine understanding. The aim of this short study is not to provide a set of ready-made views: it aims to introduce a fascinating and important period in British history, to stimulate further reading and, above all, to encourage students to think critically how best to formulate judgements for themselves.

2
Labour's apprenticeship

When Victory in Europe was achieved in May 1945 the prestige of Winston Churchill stood toweringly high. Not only had he stood out in the late 1930s against the 'guilty men' who appeased Hitler, but he had led Britain through 'blood, toil, tears and sweat' to final victory. And yet, when in his first election broadcast this great orator warned that a Labour government would ultimately introduce some form of Gestapo, few took him seriously. Such scare tactics had in the past produced tangible effects, but in July 1945 Labour was elected to power for the first time. The party's success probably owed very little to the election campaign itself. It was the culmination of almost half a century of history.

The party had been formed in February 1900, though the name Labour party was not officially adopted until six years later. Labour was to provide independent working-class representation at Westminster. Despite the fact that large numbers of working men, and all women, were unable to vote – so that there were at most 100 seats in the whole country where wage-earners formed a majority of the electorate – the new party made immediate progress. At the election of 1906 it won 29 seats, and in 1910 its total increased to about 40. But there seemed no chance of Labour's challenging for power within the foreseeable future, especially since, from 1909, the Liberal government adopted ambitious social reforms which seemed likely to gain working-class support.

In 1914 Labour was planning to contest 150 seats at the next election, twice as many as ever before but still less than a quarter of all constituencies. By this stage the party was certainly a long way from forming a proper opposition, let alone a government. It did not have the support of all trade unionists, while only a minority of workers were in a trade union, and on issues that were of no concern to industry many of its MPs failed to take an interest or register a vote. Future progress, as Gordon Phillips has recently written, was likely to be 'slow and piece-meal, rather than sudden and spectacular'. Indeed, in the summer of 1914 regression seemed more likely, for at the start of the First World War, as British men flocked to enlist, several prominent Labour leaders opposed the call to arms and favoured a general strike to bring the capitalists to their senses.

A fatal split in the party was avoided and, paradoxically, the war of 1914–18 provided favourable conditions for the growth of Labour. In return for a no-strike agreement Labour men were taken into government, Arthur Henderson even serving as a member of the war cabinet in 1916–17. The established parties paid the price for the support of the working classes – without which the war could not be won – by taking Labour into government. The number of trade unionists also grew substantially. In addition, at the end of the war the franchise was extended to all men over 21 and all women over 30, virtually trebling the electorate. Of equal significance was the fact that the Liberal party was divided by the war. In December 1916 Lloyd George had replaced Asquith as Prime Minister, and this change produced a fatal schism. But, regardless of personalities, Liberalism was falling apart; the nature of the war, lasting for years and demanding the regimentation of society, was proving fatal to Liberal ideology. Labour, however, found state direction and control much more in keeping with its outlook. In addition, party organisers managed to hammer out an effective party constitution in 1918.

This new programme, *Labour and the New Social Order*, not only improved organisational structure – so that individual membership was allowed – but enumerated a set of objectives that gave the party a new and distinctive identity. Hitherto Labour had been doctrinally virginal, having as its central purpose simply the return of MPs to Westminster. Now it became an avowedly 'socialist' party, pledging itself to produce a society based not on conflict and inequality but on 'deliberately planned co-operation in production and distribution'. In the words of Clause IV, the aim of the party was

> to secure for the producers by hand or by brain the full fruits of their industry and the most equitable distribution thereof that may be possible, upon the basis of the Common Ownership of the Means of Production and the best obtainable system of popular administration and control of each industry and service.

Socialism, according to this definition, meant not private ownership and free market capitalism, which bred inequality and exploitation, but public ownership and state direction of the economy. But in fact this statement of principles did not adequately define the outlook of even the intellectual wing of the Labour party. If for some socialism was essentially an economic doctrine necessitating nationalisation, for others it was primarily ethical, with the stress on liberty, the brotherhood of man and the moral regeneration of the individual. For the first group what mattered was collectivism, state control and bureaucratic efficiency; but the second group, while anticapitalist, was equally against state collectivism. This was an important difference of aim, but there were divisions too over method. Some believed that the socialist goal could only come about swiftly, and perhaps violently, as a result of a revolution; but far more Labour supporters, including the Fabians, thought it would occur slowly, almost imperceptibly, with 'the inevitability of gradualness'.

It should also be remembered that for many more Labour party supporters, outside the realms of the intellectuals, 'socialism' expressed simply an ill-defined desire to achieve better living conditions and greater equality of income and opportunity. They used the word in a rhetorical, vaguely emotive and imprecise sense. Most trade unionists were inclined to this usage. The unions were the dominant element in the party, providing the funds without which it could not survive, and they tended to be impatient of theorising. Although groups like the miners were calling for the nationalisation of their industries as the best means of securing better conditions, most unionists

8

were predominantly interested in the preservation or extension of trade union rights in the law and the improvement of working conditions. Their aims revolved around the solution of immediate problems, so that the far vista of a wholly reformed society meant little to them. Their basic attitudes and programme were 'labourism' rather than socialism.

Clearly Labour was a coalition – and in some ways a very uneasy alliance – between disparate groups. The party attracted a mass following and also small but growing numbers of intellectuals. Its supporters included libertarians and collectivists, pragmatists and theorists. They wanted everything from a classless society to piecemeal improvements in working conditions and preached everything from class-warfare to class-collaboration. The fact that Labour was a very 'broad church', drawing inspiration from Christ as well as Marx, gave the party a great width of appeal, but it did not make for unity or cohesion. The 1918 programme certainly did not unite these disparate elements. To some Clause IV was an immediate aim, to others it *might* have relevance in the dim and distant future, while to many it was simply mythology to which lip-service might occasionally be paid. Some considered Labour to be a party of social reform – rather like the Liberals, many of whom were soon deserting a sinking party for one obviously on the rise – and aimed to achieve change within the existing framework of society. Others saw it as a socialist party, with the aim of producing a new form of society.

In the interwar years Labour experienced contrasting fortunes. Initially all went well. In 1918 the first election for almost ten years produced a breakthrough. (The next ten-year gap, 1935–45, was to produce even more seismic changes.) In 1918 Labour fielded more candidates and won more seats than ever before. In the 1920s its progress was remarkable, from 22 per cent of the popular vote in 1918 to 37 per cent in 1929. Labour took over as the Liberals declined in working-class constituencies. Small wonder that the party's supporters were buoyed up with the confident assumption that the future lay with them: capitalism would, at some time in the future, inevitably be replaced by socialism. Even so, there were still problems to overcome. Ramsay MacDonald, leader from 1922, saw two vital areas for improvement. First, Labour was identified too exclusively with the industrial working class and the trade unions. Seeing a vital difference between a party of protest and a potential governing party, he wished Labour to be a truly national grouping, drawing support from all progressives in the community. Second, he was aware that Labour was not widely trusted and that wild rumours were circulating to the effect that if it were ever to take office it would prove totally incompetent – or worse. Could such a party be expected to defend Britain adequately? Would it not prove to be the pawn of the unions? In addition, Labour was damned by association with the Bolshevik revolution of 1917, so that some doubted whether the party was truly democratic.

After the election of December 1923 Labour had the chance to form a minority government. Not even the largest single party, it would be in office but not in power. Yet MacDonald seized his opportunity to gain executive experience and to show the nation that Labour was fit to govern. In this way he hoped to give the lie to the exaggerated rumours and, as a result, to attract more voters to the cause in the future. This strategy worked successfully, at least in part. The first Labour government lasted only nine months, but at the next election the party gained another million votes. Ministers took the advice of their civil servants and showed their general competence; they even, with Wheatley's Housing Act, showed a degree of creativity. In fact Labour did not have to *do* anything at all while in office: it simply had to avoid the wild actions its critics had predicted. Yet in fact political adversaries still managed to see sinister, pro-Soviet designs behind this respectable facade, and the 1924 election campaign was marked by the 'red scare', the Zinoviev letter. Nevertheless, Labour's march was still onward and upward. Even the General Strike of 1926, from which Mac-Donald hastily dissociated himself, aided the cause: henceforth trade unionists pinned their hopes for reform on the Labour party rather than on discredited 'direct action'.

In 1929 came the formation of the second Labour government. Still without a majority, and indeed polling fewer votes than the Conservatives, Labour was now at least the largest single party in the Commons. At this rate a majority government would not be far distant. But in 1931 Labour left office ignominiously and went into opposition, being replaced by a coalition, the National government, led by Labour's two best-known figures, Prime Minister MacDonald and Chancellor of the Exchequer Philip Snowden. At the subsequent election all the old scare stories were revived. In October 1931 Snowden described the programme of his former party as 'Bolshevism run mad'. Labour seats declined catastrophically from 288 to 52. The root cause of Labour's failure was its inability to grapple with the Great Depression. Labour theorists had long believed that capitalism needed the scourge of unemployment to keep wage levels down: capitalism therefore meant unemployment, just as surely as it meant class-war and war between nations. They also knew that under socialism such evils would not exist. What they had not worked out was how to convert the old system into the new. Certainly they had little idea how to grapple with rising unemployment within a capitalist society. In short, the second Labour government was composed of poor capitalists and equally poor socialists. Ministers were too orthodox to be socialist and too socialist to be orthodox. They dithered until, in 1931, they were presented with the stark choice of either cutting unemployment benefit or resigning. MacDonald was all for making cuts: he had always believed that in office Labour had to act in the interests of the whole nation, even to the extent of taking actions unpopular with its traditional voters. Henderson, on the other hand, with the backing of the TUC, refused to countenance cuts in the dole: the unemployed were 'our people'. Personal animosity between Henderson and MacDonald was thus exacerbated because each represented different strands of Labour ideology. (Their equivalents in 1951 were Nye Bevan and Hugh Gaitskell.) With the cabinet split down the middle, MacDonald resigned as Labour premier and, to the shock of most of his colleagues, headed the Tory-dominated National government.

The 1931 crisis was a calamity for Labour. It was not so much the ending of the party's period in office, or the defection of MacDonald, which so shocked Labour supporters: it was the enormity of their defeat in the 1931 election. Labour's progress had hitherto been steadily upward, but no longer was it possible to be confident that the future lay with them. The result was a period of introspection and reconstruction which has attracted considerable historical debate. How thoroughgoing was Labour's theoretical stocktaking and how fundamentally did the party change? Certainly there could be no homogeneous response, given the party's pronounced heterogeneity. In some ways it seemed that the party was moving definitely to the left. Labour soon decided that it would never again accept office merely for the sake of office; instead it would introduce 'definite socialist legislation immediately'. There were even some, especially in the Socialist League formed by Stafford Cripps, who thought that the capitalist class would never voluntarily give up its privileges and that Labour would have to introduce constitutional reform, including emergency legislation to rule by decree. Since evolution no longer guaranteed success, a boost was given to notions of revolutionary socialism. Yet despite this proliferation of new ideas, the left did not capture control of the party.

One lesson drawn from 1931 was that henceforth the leader of the party should be a less dominant figure than the brilliant but aloof and untrustworthy MacDonald. The débâcle of the 1931 election left few available candidates in the parliamentary party. The aged George Lansbury was chosen in 1931 but had to resign because, as a pacifist, he opposed the use of sanctions in 1935. Clement Attlee then took over, representative of a new generation that dominated Labour until the end of the 1940s. Attlee was the most senior of the available candidates and, perhaps his most outstanding characteristic, he was as unlike MacDonald as possible. Critics called him bland and timid – 'a little mouse' who preferred to follow rather than lead. But, after Ramsay MacDonald, these personal characteristics were seen by many as virtues rather than vices. Unless acquiescence in the views of the majority conflicted with his conscience, wrote Attlee in 1936, he would 'fall into line'. Ideologically, he favoured moderate socialism, as indeed did his rivals for the leadership, Herbert Morrison and Arthur Greenwood.

Under Attlee, Labour became more closely associated with the trade unions and thus with the moderate reformism of union leaders like Ernest Bevin. But the party also worked out a series of short-term policies to be implemented immediately it came to office, thus remedying the main weakness of the second Labour government. For instance, instead of indulging in generalised rhetoric about social ownership, it pledged itself to nationalise specific industries. Never again would Labour combine utopian long-term aims with conservative short-term actions. Even so, it was uncertain whether a Labour government, on these policies, would be improving the existing capitalist system or replacing it with a new socialist structure. There was still an ambiguity about the real aims and nature of the party.

Fascism in Europe, and Chamberlain's controversial policy of appeasement, meant that foreign, rather than domestic, policy was the key area of debate after 1935. Yet while Labour theorists were clear that the ultimate culprit, because the ultimate cause of war, was capitalism itself, they were less clear on what policies they should advance to cope with aggressors in the pre-socialist era. Outright pacifism was rejected. But for a long time Labour tried to combine the incompatible – collective security with disarmament. Only gradually, as the 1930s wore on and as the threat posed by Hitler became more stark, did Labour leaders realise that they had to deal with the world as it was, not as they might wish it to be. The leadership eventually overcame the party's reluctance to sanction rearmament, even under the existing government.

Labour put its house in order after 1931 and gained greater electoral success. In the 1935 election it secured 154 seats, with an increase in its popular vote from 30 to 38 per cent. Nevertheless, by 1939 the party was in a quandary. It had growing support in the country but, even so, seemed unlikely to win a general election. The defection of its leading personalities to the National government in 1931 had left it with a front-bench team almost devoid of governmental experience. People would be loath to elect a government without proven ministerial competence, and yet such experience could not be gained without prior electoral success. In 1923 the impasse had been solved by good fortune, in that parliamentary deadlock had allowed a minority government to come to office, but Labour had ruled out taking office in similar circumstances in the future. The only other possibility seemed to be a coalition, as in the First World War; but, after the trauma of 1931, Labour was not disposed to make deals with the capitalist parties. When the Second World War started in September 1939, Labour agreed to an electoral truce – so that by-elections would not be contested by the main parties – but would not enter a coalition.

The ending of the Phoney War in April 1940 transformed British politics and Labour's fortunes. Chamberlain, who had long treated Labour as dirt, could no longer command the support of the Commons and was replaced by Churchill. Labour played a key role in this. Chamberlain's only hope of remaining

13

Prime Minister was to form a coalition, but whereas Attlee – after consulting the party executive – made known Labour's willingness to enter a coalition, he insisted that this would only be under a new premier. It was a wise decision. The year 1940 marked a turning point for the party.

There are obvious reasons why Labour's position was boosted in the years 1940–5. Clearly the very nature of the war – total war, in which, as Churchill said, the fronts were everywhere, so that workmen were soldiers with different weapons but the same courage – necessitated state direction of the economy. No industries were nationalised – that would have been too politically divisive – but almost the whole economy came under state direction and control. Britain saw 'war socialism' to an even greater extent than in 1914–18. While the Conservatives saw their private enterprise philosophy shelved, Labour's collectivism was implemented. Not everyone approved of this new regime, certainly not those conscripted to mine coal in the pits; but most people accepted that it was necessary and welcomed its benefits, including high levels of employment and increased real wages.

Wartime experiences were of seminal importance for Labour's victory in July 1945. People now began to see the previous decades in a new light. In the 1930s many had accepted the view of Conservative politicians that governments could not create jobs and that therefore mass unemployment, while regrettable, was inevitable. Now the state created millions of jobs. The 1930s, a time of prosperity for most people, became in retrospect the 'hungry thirties' of needlessly wasted lives. Clearly, if full employment was to be maintained after the war, there could be no return to unfettered private enterprise. Even *The Times* insisted, in 1940, that democracy did not deserve the name if it maintained the right to vote but forgot the right to work. In short, the war saw a remarkable shift of opinion to the left; and it was in vain that right-wing Conservatives, seeking scapegoats for this political transformation, blamed the poisoning of innocent minds by groups like the Army Bureau of Current Affairs. Nor could they damn Labour by association with the Soviet Union, now transformed by Hitler's Operation Barbarossa into a gallant ally.

Labour undoubtedly gained politically during the war. In fact, as Marwick has argued, it gained a 'double dividend':

14

Labour men were part of the government, so gaining experience and recognition, but they were never fully identified with it and so gained popularity for being more progressive than the Tories. Labour was in the enviable position of being simultaneously government and opposition. This was shown most clearly in the debate over the Beveridge plan for a postwar welfare state. Beveridge called for a comprehensive insurance scheme which would provide subsistence benefits 'from the cradle to the grave'. The government reluctantly accepted the plan in principle, Labour's ministers showing themselves among the keenest for its implementation, but almost 100 Labour backbenchers voted against the government and called for a more whole-hearted commitment. Tory backbench revolts, on the other hand, were usually against 'progressive' causes.

Undoubtedly there was a consensus during the war. Had there not been, the coalition could not have functioned. The common enemy led British politicians to emphasise what united, not what divided, them. Nevertheless 'consensus' is a relative not an absolute term. There were important differences of emphasis between the Labour and Conservative parties towards the end of the war. The reform programmes that were agreed tended, as Jeffreys has argued, to be of the 'lowest common denominator' type, representing the least that Labour would accept and the most that the Conservatives would countenance.

Labour gained more than ideological advantage from the war. The party also emerged, by 1945, with a formidable front-bench team of ministers. Perhaps the most popular was Ernest Bevin, the trade union leader who before the war had not even been an MP. He served as a remarkably successful Minister of Labour and National Service from 1940 to 1945. Herbert Morrison was Minister of Supply in 1940 before coming into his own as Home Secretary. Dalton was Minister of Economic Warfare from 1940 to 1942 and then President of the Board of Trade until 1945. Several other Labour men also held key and prominent positions, including Cripps. One man who did not hit the headlines was party leader Clement Attlee. He served as a member of the war cabinet for the duration of the coalition – the only man other than Churchill to do so – and as Deputy Prime Minister from 1942 to 1945. But some colleagues found him uninspiring – and an American journalist called him at this time the 'dullest man in English politics'. Some years later a civil servant, comparing Churchill and Attlee as prime ministers, judged that the differences between the two men were extraordinary: 'On the one side, decision, firm answers, everything down just like that – bang, bang. And on the other side, hesitation, uncertainty . . .' It was Attlee who was the figure of firmness! Several perceptive observers also compared favourably the Labour leader's chairmanship of the cabinet with that of Churchill, for whom he often deputised. Churchill would treat ministers to interminable monologues of impeccably phrased prose. Ministers went home, in the early hours of the morning, 'feeling we have been present at an historic occasion'; but in fact nothing had been decided. It was the terse Attlee who ensured that business was despatched rapidly: ministers kept to the agenda, made decisions and went home in reasonable time. Certainly Churchill recognised Attlee's contribution to the war effort, once going so far as to say that although he was 'not a man with whom it is agreeable to dine' there was none of his Labour colleagues for whom he had more respect. The public heard little of this good work behind the scenes, but at least Attlee seemed trustworthy and respectable. This inoffensive little man was himself the perfect response to Churchill's fatheaded Gestapo slur.

Labour had far fewer ministers than the Conservatives during the war but their work was concentrated on domestic matters, and in particular they took an interest in reconstruction, the issue – or, rather, cluster of issues – of most concern to the electorate. Churchill, in picking Labour men for their posts, had contributed enormously to their victory in 1945. In contrast, few Conservatives made a name for themselves during the war. In addition the Tories had to bear the stigma for the failures of the interwar period – especially appeasement and mass unemployment. 'Never again' and 'You can't trust the Tories' were effective slogans during the election. Their trump card was Churchill himself, but to many this political maverick seemed a figure almost without party affiliation. Others reckoned that, while the right man for the war, he would make a poor peacetime premier. Churchill may have voiced the feelings of the nation in the dark days of 1940, but this was probably the first and last occasion on which he did so. By the end of the war he was badly out of touch with the national mood. The result was Labour's great victory in July 1945.

Left-wingers like Aneurin (Nye) Bevan had feared that Labour leaders would be meekly subservient in the coalition to Churchill. They were proved wrong. Bevan had also worried that, as an arm of the coalition, Labour would lose its socialist passion to transform society and become merely a party of social reform. Was he equally wrong in this view? When in 1944 the coalition pledged itself to maintain a 'high and stable level' of employment after the war, Bevan was indignant. In his view, only socialism – and public ownership – could produce full employment; capitalism, even of a reformed and Keynesian kind, would sooner or later produce unemployment. If the government pledge could be made good, he reasoned with remarkable candour, then a socialist party would have no reason to exist.

'The Labour Party', proclaimed its 1945 manifesto *Let Us Face The Future*, 'is a Socialist Party, and proud of it', adding rather more equivocally that socialism could not come overnight and appealing for the support of all 'progressives'. Never before had Labour had a better chance of showing what it could do or of demonstrating exactly what its 'socialism' really amounted to.

3

Attlee and his ministers

Victory in 1945 came as a shock to many Labour politicians. How could Labour, led by the timid Attlee, have triumphed over the Conservatives, led by the charismatic war hero Churchill? Perhaps the party had won despite its leader. Immediately the results became known Attlee was urged to stand for re-election by the Parliamentary Labour Party (PLP) before accepting George VI's invitation to form a government. Here was a scarcely veiled attempt to replace him by a 'bigger' personality as party leader and thus as Prime Minister. Attlee had led the party since 1935, but many had regarded his appointment as provisional and now thought his period as caretaker had gone on quite long enough. Attlee, however, ignored the advice and formed a government. He did not worry over others' doubts about his ability. He did not listen to political gossip and consulted the press mainly for the cricket scores and *The Times* crossword. Perhaps he was unaware of some of the choicer criticisms. It was said, for instance, that when Attlee joined Stalin and Truman, replacing Churchill at Potsdam, the Big Three became the Big Two-and-a-Half. Bevan wrote that Attlee was determined to make a trumpet sound like a tin-whistle, and George Orwell compared him to 'a recently dead fish, before it has had time to stiffen'. *The Economist* once wrote that the arid and uninspiring Attlee 'touches nothing that he does not dehydrate'. One wit told the story of the arrival at

18

10 Downing Street of an empty taxi, out of which emerged Mr Attlee.

Such caricatures were grossly unfair. Admittedly Attlee was not flamboyant and had few oratorical skills. He was inclined to answer press questions with a simple 'yes' or 'no' or 'I don't know'. Nor did he have any real capacity to inspire: ministers were inclined to think that, while he might well rap them over the knuckles for errors, they were very unlikely to receive any praise. He was seen as a rather inaccessible and daunting schoolmaster or as an impartial umpire rather than the captain of a team. He was in fact a shy man. When an assistant whip admitted to feeling nervous before a speech, Attlee commented: 'Don't worry, I'm *always* nervous.' He found it difficult to exchange cheery greetings with ministers and backbenchers and had no small talk. A junior minister has recalled that the Prime Minister had to 'screw himself up' just to say good morning. No wonder he never used one word when none would do. Yet this diffidence was not a sign of any lack of confidence in his own judgement. Indeed, some people found him rather arrogant. Inside the meek and undemonstrative Clement Attlee there was a dominant and assertive man struggling to get out.

It is often said that Attlee lacked any real understanding of economics. This was true (and equally true of most of his predecessors as premier, and not a few of his successors); but at least he had the humility to recognise deficiencies and take the advice of those better qualified than himself. He was in this, as in so many respects, the antithesis of Ramsay MacDonald. He once mused that it is always a mistake to think yourself bigger than you are. Attlee's self-knowledge ruled out this error. He combined considerable abilities with habits of hard work. As a result he was always well-informed, and everyone recognised that he was solid and efficient. Above all, he was an excellent chairman of cabinet with a remarkable ability to get through an agenda and, when necessary, to silence over-talkative colleagues. Democracy means government by discussion; but Attlee was aware that unless people know when to stop talking democracy can degenerate into discussion without government.

Attlee's political position tended to be in the centre of his party. Certainly he was a reformer, with a genuine concern to improve the lot of the poor. He had entered politics by way of social work in the East End of London; appalled at avoidable poverty, he wished to see a more caring and more equal society. Yet while wanting change, he was also in many ways a conservative figure, a product of public school and Oxford and of the late-Victorian era. He was even said to shudder when the port was passed round the dining table the wrong way. He therefore stood for stability as well as reform and may be seen as personifying Labour's essential ambiguity of aim and outlook.

Attlee proved the doubters wrong. He survived as Prime Minister for six years, and his reputation stood much higher at the end of this period than at the beginning. The teacher had been promoted in popular esteem: the *Observer* in 1950 saw him as 'a great headmaster, controlled, efficient and, above all, good'. 'Waspish' was an adjective often applied to him after 1945: the opposition in debates, as well as some of his own colleagues, found that the seemingly inoffensive little man could deliver a sharp sting. A journalist once wrote that the parliamentary duel between Attlee and Churchill was like a contest in a bullring: Attlee was the small and nimble toreador 'teasing and infuriating his magnificent opponent with his sudden barbs'.

Attlee was not the greatest Prime Minister this country has ever had. Yet he was anything but the mediocrity his critics alleged. Many historians have rated him among the best postwar premiers and Labour's best so far, though the notion that he was a 'poor man's Baldwin' has not been entirely laid to rest. Almost certainly no one else could have done a better job in 1945–51, though some wished to try. There were moves to unseat him in 1945 and again in 1947 and 1949, but such attempts came nowhere near succeeding. Partly this was due to Ernest Bevin, who showed remarkable loyalty; partly it was the result of Attlee's own skill, especially in 1947 when he adroitly neutralised one of the conspirators, Stafford Cripps, by promoting him. Above all it was due to the fact that his rivals were divided among themselves, disliking each other more than Attlee. The Prime Minister did not need to 'divide and rule'. The divisions already existed; Attlee's job was to prevent them widening into splits. He himself had very few enemies in the PLP. Being associated with no particular faction or wing of the party, he did not offend any of the others. He was neither 'left' nor 'right'. Only he, it has been well said, could have presided over the prima donnas in his cabinet.

One of these was Ernest Bevin, the creator of the Transport

and General Workers' Union, who had been catapulted into parliament and ministerial office in 1940. In 1945 Attlee, who had considered making him Chancellor, appointed him Foreign Secretary instead. Bevin was a man of great powers and of great egotism. It has been said that he did not so much represent the trade unions as embody them, and their backing gave him enormous power within the cabinet. No one, even his enemies, doubted his abilities. A blunt man who could at times seem like a bully, he was also highly imaginative and an administrator of outstanding skill. He has been called the finest negotiator of his generation. One drawback to his career after 1945 was his health. Towards the end of the war his doctor judged that there was no sound organ in his 18-stone body apart from his feet. He later said that Bevin suffered from angina pectoris, cardiac failure, arteriosclerosis, sinusitis, enlarged liver, damaged kidneys and high blood pressure. A private detective was usually on hand with a box of pills (referred to by Bevin as his 'pellets') for use if his heart condition gave cause for alarm. But he refused to alter his lifestyle. He overworked and took little exercise. He also smoked and drank too much, one of his secretaries saying that he used alcohol as a car uses petrol. Herbert Morrison once walked out of a meeting of ministers complaining at Bevin's 'drunken monologue'. Bevin's other main weakness was that he took criticisms personally, often as a 'stab in the back', and made enemies very easily. He and Attlee were opposites who attracted, but with Morrison, another self-made man, he got on particularly badly. One reason Attlee sent Bevin to the Foreign Office was to minimise clashes with Morrison, who, as Leader of the House of Commons and Lord President of the Council, had overall responsibility for domestic affairs. These two men had to be kept as far apart as possible.

Herbert Morrison had been a successful Leader of the London County Council in the 1930s, when the Webbs referred to him as a 'Fabian of Fabians', and an equally successful Home Secretary during the war. A shrewd party manager, he had been the leading figure behind Labour's 1945 election strategy and had virtually written its manifesto. It was due to his skill that a record number of bills was piloted through the Commons in Labour's first years; and the nationalisation programme in particular bore his stamp. A tremendously hard worker with few interests outside politics, he seemed to have a finger in every

21

political pie. His oversight of economic affairs may have won him few plaudits, but he felt he had far more ability than Attlee and deserved the premiership himself. It was not surprising, therefore, when in 1947 he refused to support a move led by Dalton and Cripps to press for Bevin's elevation. As Prime Minister himself, he would have met with the hostility of several other ministers. Dalton got on badly with him, and Nye Bevan disliked his cautious approach to policy, calling him a 'fifth-rate Tammany boss'. Bevin, with rather less subtlety, referred to 'That little bugger 'Erbert'.

Attlee's choice as Chancellor was Hugh Dalton. Educated at Eton and King's College, Cambridge, the product of a wealthy and privileged background, Dalton seemed a class traitor to his Conservative enemies. They said he took to socialism out of a desire for revenge on the wealthy classes. It was a role in which he delighted: he imposed redistributive taxation with a proverbial song in his heart, wanting to reduce inequality not at some indeterminate time in the future but immediately, and he attacked the Tories in the Commons with panache and verve. His biographer, Ben Pimlott, judges him to be the only distinctively socialist Chancellor of the Exchequer Britain has ever seen. He was certainly one of the few ministers determined that steel should be nationalised. Highly critical of Attlee and with a love of political intrigue, he certainly thought someone else should be Prime Minister.

Dalton's own case for the premiership was not good. He had a reputation for insincerity which could not be shaken off – largely because it was all too true – and some found him positively sly. He also talked too much and too loudly: it was said that his whispers carried hundreds of yards. The story was told that if he had become Foreign Secretary, as he wished in 1945, secret diplomacy would have ended forthwith. Small wonder that he made enemies quite effortlessly. Morrison referred to him as a 'bugger' and Bevin talked of 'that bastard Dalton', intimating all too clearly what he should do with himself. Estranged from his wife and with a fondness for younger men, he lacked Attlee's stable home life. Perhaps as a consequence, he found it hard to relax and to survive the strains of high office. A variety of psychosomatic ailments, including painful boils, afflicted him at times of particular stress. During the crises of 1947 he was taking benzedrine pills, which German soldiers used to take before going into battle, and, temporarily, feeling much better. In November 1947 he foolishly revealed details of his budget to a reporter and resigned. It was only a very minor infringement of parliamentary etiquette and he could have survived. But he offered his resignation because he wished to go, and Attlee accepted to get rid of him. Out of office, his ailments miraculously disappeared. When he returned to government the following year, he was no longer a political heavyweight.

The final member of the 'Big Five' was Sir Stafford Cripps. He replaced Dalton as Chancellor, having served as President of the Board of Trade in 1945-7 and, briefly, as Minister of Economic Affairs in 1947. As soon as he became Chancellor Cripps was identified with the economic austerity which marked the late 1940s. A puritanical figure, he seemed to delight in the mortific-ation of British flesh. A vegetarian who dined on apple juice and raw asparagus – as well as a workaholic, rising at four in the morning to get in three hours' work before a cold bath, after which the daily grind would begin in earnest – he seemed to personify austerity. He was the sort of man who favoured shorter skirts for women – and thus disliked the 'New Look' – but only because of the material that would thereby be saved. Few doubted his ability, least of all Cripps himself: he came to think of himself as the next Prime Minister. Yet many doubted his common sense. He was now a convert to orthodox political economy, but before the war he had been an equally zealous Marxist. In 1939, Dalton had written that Cripps 'has all the political judgement of a flea'. After 1945 he was a hero to some MPs, including puritanical Tories like Cyril Osborne, but others found his high-mindedness rather sanctimonious. 'There but for the grace of God', quipped Churchill, 'goes God'. Everyone knew exactly what he meant.

In the words of Harold Macmillan, the cabinet from 1945 constituted 'a body of ministers as talented as any in the history of Parliament'. Of the 'Big Five' politicians, Attlee seemed to have least ability, and yet only he could have ruled over the others. When someone once said of Nye Bevan that he was his own worst enemy, Bevin retorted: 'Not while I'm alive, he ain't'. Variations on this story are common: maybe it was Morrison who issued the retort, or perhaps Bevin said it of Morrison or of Shinwell. Or was it Morrison of Dalton? In fact any combination is possible. But not quite. Certainly Attlee would never have said it of anyone; nor would anyone ever have said it of him. Brendan Bracken judged correctly in 1948 that so long as his colleagues were fighting each other, Attlee would be certain to remain Prime Minister. But not only did he remain at Number Ten; Clement Attlee also managed to weld his cabinet into a very constructive and effective team.

The average age of the cabinet in 1945 was 60 (compared with 43 for Labour MPs as a whole). The Big Five elder statesmen were all born within a few years of each other, and most came to show increasing signs of physical and emotional strain as the government proceeded. Many Labour ministers had indeed been carrying the burdens of office continuously since 1940. Morrison was in hospital suffering from a thrombosis that threatened his life in February and March 1947; Attlee was in hospital in August and September 1948, and also in March 1951, with a duodenal ulcer; Bevin's health was notoriously bad and he died – characteristically, with a box of official papers on his lap – in 1951; Dalton's health was poor; and Cripps had to resign in 1950. Was there an infusion of younger blood during these years? Perhaps not as much as there might have been. Nevertheless, several younger men were promoted. Harold Wilson entered the cabinet as President of the Board of Trade in 1947 at the age of only 31, Patrick Gordon Walker as Commonwealth Secretary in 1950 aged 43. But the two key younger figures were Aneurin Bevan, who became Minister of Health in 1945 at the age of 48, and Hugh Gaitskell, who became Minister of Fuel and Power in 1947, when he was 41, and Chancellor of the Exchequer in succession to Cripps in 1950.

Bevan was the odd man out in Attlee's cabinet for several reasons. The working-class background of this Welsh radical was not unusual, but his outlook was. He was a 'fundamentalist', believing more passionately than any of his colleagues that socialism meant not mere piecemeal reform but the transformation of society. He, alone of the cabinet, acknowledged a major intellectual debt to Marx. He did not wish to see the nationalisation of the whole of the means of production, distribution and exchange, but he did think that in a 'mixed economy' the public sector should be dominant. Private industry would be merely the 'light cavalry' in the nation's economic forces. Many believed that, with ideas like this, his natural role in parliament was as a backbench critic, and certainly during the war he had been a persistent critic of Churchill (or, as Churchill preferred to call him, a 'squalid nuisance'). He was also the only man in Labour ranks who could match Churchill's oratorical skills, although Bevan was an orator of a very different stamp – as conversational and improvised as Churchill was rhetorical and rehearsed. The choice of the inexperienced Bevan for the Ministry of Health in 1945 was certainly Attlee's most daring appointment. It was also one of his most successful, for Bevan proved a highly competent and constructive minister. The inauguration of the National Health Service in 1948, arguably Labour's greatest achievement, owed much to him. His record on house-building was also substantial. The firebrand had an unexpected capacity for compromise and conciliation, together with real administrative flair.

But Bevan was a firebrand none the less. In 1948 he referred to Tories as 'lower than vermin', a phrase which the press (recently described by him as 'the most prostituted in the world') seized on and kept alive until the next election. Bevan was not worried about alienating Conservatives or the middle classes. Indeed, a socialist government, to his mind, was not doing its job properly if reactionary sectors were not howling. Labour's natural supporters were the working classes, and it was their good opinions and votes which he sought. With their backing, another Labour government would be elected.

His polar opposite in the cabinet was Herbert Morrison, who believed that Labour would only be re-elected if it won a proportion of middle-class votes. After a period of radical change, he wished to pause rather than embark on further reforms. As early as 1946 he told Labour's annual conference that the government had gone 'as far Left as is consistent with sound reason and the national interest'. In 1948 his recipe for victory was 'consolidation'. Rather than nationalise further industries, Labour should make sure that those already taken into public ownership were working well and in the public interest. As the next election loomed closer, Morrison and Bevan espoused widely differing strategies. Bevan was not against caution at times. Neither Rome nor the New Jerusalem could be built in a day. In 1945 he had insisted that socialists could not do in five years all that needed to be done: twenty-five would be a more realistic figure. There was, to his mind, no 'immaculate conception of socialism'. Yet Morrison seemed after 1947 to be so gradualist that it was hard for Bevan to see that he wanted to go forward at all. Morrison's critics said he believed that sound administration was the cure of all the ills to which flesh was heir; and indeed he had once said that his supreme ambition in life was 'the achievement of tidiness'. After a tussle with Morrison, Bevan once complained: 'It is a form of torture unknown to the ancients to be compelled on the last Wednesday of every month to convert the leaders of the Labour Party afresh to the most elementary principles.'

Strife within the government had for several years been muted: ministers had been too busy carrying out reforms to argue for long among themselves. But by 1949 Labour, having successfully implemented the aims agreed at the end of the war, began to turn to those on which it was not agreed. Intra-party debate produced a manifesto for the 1950 election which was permeated with Morrison's gradualist approach, but with the addition of a watered-down, Bevanite 'shopping list' of candidates for nationalisation, including cement and shipbuilding. The result was a close-run contest between Labour and Conservatives: Labour's vote went up by 1.25 million, so that for the second time running they received more votes than any previous political party, but their proportion of the total vote fell slightly. There was a 2.8 per cent swing to the Tories. Labour lost 78 seats compared with 1945, the Conservatives gained 85. Overall, Labour had a working majority, but only of five. It was, wrote Dalton, the 'worst possible situation . . . office without authority or power'. Here was electoral grist for the strategic mills of both Morrison and Bevan. Morrison could point to evidence, including the loss of seats in southern England, that the middle-class vote had deserted Labour. He therefore judged that the party should adopt a less threatening and more moderate, consolidationist approach. Bevan, on the other hand, could insist that the middle classes were natural Tories and that Labour should redouble its efforts to appeal to its natural allies, the working classes, around 30 per cent of whom were still voting Conservative.

The scene seemed set, after the election, for further battles between these two men. But it was not to be. Morrison was appointed Foreign Secretary after Bevin's ill health forced his removal, and in this unaccustomed and very challenging role – in which he did not prove a success – he was removed from direct confrontation with Bevan. Hugh Gaitskell stepped into his shoes and a battle occurred which he considered a 'fight for the soul of the Labour Party'.

Gaitskell, educated at Winchester and New College, Oxford, came from a background very different from that of the ex-miner from Tredegar. But their temperaments were even further apart. Dalton described Gaitskell as a 'high snow peak', while Bevan was a 'steaming tropical swamp'. Gaitskell seemed un-emotional and highly self-controlled, a typical civil servant according to the Welshman Bevan who was much given to speaking his mind and whose thought, according to his critics, began in his mouth. Yet their differences were more than merely personal. Bevan believed that intellectuals like Gaitskell, with no real roots in the party, did not understand ordinary working people. He feared that under such figures as the new Chancellor 'socialism' would degenerate into soulless administrative effic-iency. Gaitskell, on the other hand, insisted that Labour had to be a coalition of different interests and should not be merely a one-class party, especially not a party devoted to a class which was rapidly losing its traditional character and becoming more diverse. He believed that the party should be modernised, and he was later to urge that Clause IV be dropped from its constitu-tion. If Bevan was a 'fundamentalist' and Morrison a 'con-solidationist', Gaitskell tended to be a 'revisionist'. He judged that Bevan's emotional approach to politics might render Labour unelectable.

It is difficult to believe that ambition played no part in their squabbles. Attlee was 67 in 1950, and deputy Prime Minister Morrison was only a few years younger. Who would eventually take over the mantle of leadership? Bevan was clearly a con-tender. He never indulged in petty intrigue, and some have said that he was not personally ambitious, but he clearly thought he deserved promotion, eventually to the premiership. He had been Minister of Health since 1945, and perhaps Attlee should have promoted him earlier. But when he was moved, in January 1951, it was hard to see this as real advancement. He became Minister of Labour and National Service. This was a more important post than many historians have been prepared to admit, in view of the outbreak of hostilities in Korea in June

27

1950 and the likelihood of major warfare, which according to the War Office was 'possible in 1951, probable in 1952'. But Bevan only accepted the post with great reluctance. He would have liked to succeed Bevin at the Foreign Office or, failing that, to go to the Colonial Office. The Treasury would not have been particularly appealing; but he had heard with 'consternation and astonishment' the news that Gaitskell had been appointed in October 1950. By this time there were two possible future leaders for the party, but the star of Gaitskell was rising much more rapidly in the political firmament than that of Bevan, however brightly his light burned in parliamentary debates and among the constituency parties.

An issue soon arose which highlighted the different principles of these two rivals – the increasing costs of the Health Service at a time of escalating defence expenditure. Bevan was passionately devoted to *his* NHS and particularly to the principle that all treatment should be free at the point of need. To impose charges would, to his way of thinking, be a crucial change in kind. He had got on very well with Labour's first two Chancellors, Dalton and Cripps, even though Cripps had found it necessary to insist that a small charge for prescriptions might have to be imposed. Prescription charges placed Bevan in a dilemma; but there was no certainty that they would be levied, and he decided not to be so quixotic as to resign over a mere possibility. But when Gaitskell insisted that charges would have to be imposed for half the cost of false teeth and spectacles, that was a different matter. The new Chancellor insisted that charges would save a valuable £13 million (£23 million in a full year); but Bevan insisted that such a saving was derisory, especially given a swollen defence budget of £4,700 million over the next three years. Why not make the saving from defence, especially when shortages of raw materials and of machine tools might make it impossible to spend all the money allocated? Bevan threatened to resign if the health service charges were imposed; Gaitskell promised to go if they were not. When Gaitskell received cabinet backing, Bevan hesitated and then resigned in April 1951, along with President of the Board of Trade Harold Wilson (dubbed by Dalton 'Nye's dog') and a junior minister, John Freeman.

Labour's hold on government was already tenuous, given its small majority and the poor health of several of its MPs. It was unlikely to survive for long. Resignations were therefore likely to hasten an election and to harm Labour's chances of winning. Why, then, did Bevan resign, and was he justified in doing so? Clearly he regarded the issue of payments for false teeth and spectacles as a matter of vital principle: either the NHS was free or it was not. Any charges – however limited – would destroy the basis on which he had created the Health Service and perhaps open the way for further charges. At the same time he was dismayed at the new consolidationist tenor of the Labour administration and at what he saw as the government's sub-servience to the Americans, particularly over defence spending.

On the other hand, Gaitskell and many cabinet supporters believed that the first duty of a government was to arrange for adequate armed forces: there should be no repetition of the 1930s, when Labour had for too long adopted an ostrich-like approach to foreign policy. In addition, Gaitskell was not as emotionally committed to the NHS as Bevan. If more money was available for social services, then in his view it should go to supplement old age pensions or family allowances rather than dentures and spectacles. Indeed, entries in his diary have seemed to some historians to show that he positively wished to impose charges. Sensible compromises were put forward – for instance, that NHS cuts should be postponed for six months to see if the defence budget could indeed be spent – but Gaitskell rejected them.

Could resignations have been avoided? 'Possibly' was Attlee's answer to this question; and historians cannot provide a better one. It is sometimes said that had Attlee not been in hospital, then a compromise could have been reached, especially since his deputy, Herbert Morrison, lacked the PM's conciliatory quali-ties and had little sympathy with Bevan's political outlook. But such an idea is speculative. Harold Wilson believed that the presence of Attlee would have made a difference, Patrick Gordon Walker that it would not. Certainly Attlee was consulted in hospital and talked with both the antagonists. As for the issue of who was right, Bevan or Gaitskell, every possible verdict has been reached by different writers: either, neither or both. Bevan was pictured by opponents as a new Oswald Mosley, deserting his party out of personal ambition, Gaitskell as a latter-day Philip Snowden, sacrificing both party and principles out of blind adherence to Treasury orthodoxy. Bevan seems vindicated by the fact that, as he had predicted, it proved impossible to spend all the money allotted to defence. In 1951–4 actual defence spending reached only £3,878 million, not Gaitskell's projected £4,700 million. The cuts had therefore proved unnecessary. But Gaitskell's supporters argue that hindsight was not possible for the Chancellor, that his budget was in fact well received in the Commons, that charges were fully supported by the new Health Secretary and that Bevan's erratic behaviour and ultimate inability to work as a member of a team made a showdown between the two men inevitable. Rivalry, contrasting personalities and differing political philosophies certainly made a clash extremely likely. These two men embodied the fundamentalist and reformist – or 'socialist' and 'social democratic' – strands in the Labour party, and these two philosophies were now proving hard to combine. The government's reform programme had achieved much by this time – the welfare state was in being and twenty per cent of industry had been nationalised – but this very success made it harder for the two wings of the party to cohere on the basis of an agreed programme. Labour had to make up its mind what its 'socialism' really meant.

Less speculative is an assessment of the effects of the split. The *Manchester Guardian* called the resignations an 'internal haemorrhage' from which the government was likely to bleed to death. Certainly it did no good at all for Labour's chances at the next election, in October 1951. In its manifesto Labour did not call itself a socialist party. Nor was there a shopping list of industries to be nationalised: instead Labour threatened to 'take over concerns which fail the nation', an ingenious wording that could be interpreted very differently by the left and right wings. Bevan was deliberately kept out of the limelight in the campaign. Nevertheless he did his best to minimise the political effects of his resignation and at the 1951 conference called for Labour supporters to unite and fight the election joyously, adding that he was frightened of the prospect of the warmonger Churchill ('still fighting Blenheim all over again') becoming Prime Minister in place of Clem Attlee (with his 'quiet, moderate, balanced approach'). The result was a very close-run contest. There was a 0.9 per cent swing to the Tories. Labour polled the most votes – for the third time running a new record for the number of votes cast for any political party, and one not surpassed in British psephological history until 1992 – but won fewer seats than the Conservatives. Churchill had a working majority of only seventeen. The resignations had thus not proved a catastrophe for Labour, but they may possibly have made the crucial difference between government and opposition.

At first sight, the result did not seem so bad. The slender Conservative majority seemed likely to give Labour a brief – and much needed – spell in opposition and a chance for the party to lick its wounds and return to the political fray with energy renewed. But it did not turn out that way. The party had closed ranks for the election, but defeat led to a postmortem which merely heightened doctrinal differences. Soon intra-party bickering turned into a full-scale civil war which Attlee, who retired in 1955, could do little to stop. The party did not split, but the 'Bevanites' and 'Gaitskellites' spent more time attacking each other than fighting the Tories. Instead of a brief period in opposition, Labour was to remain out of power until 1964. 1951 was followed by thirteen sterile, fratricidal years for the party. In comparison, some historians see 1945–51 as a period of relatively untroubled fraternal harmony. But to others Labour's experiences after 1951 prove that the Attlee administration had been no more than a fragile coalition, built on very superficial foundations of unity. Perhaps both views are tenable. At all events, it was the Conservative party which reaped the benefits of Labour's achievements in office.

4

Labour and the economy

Britain's survival in the Second World War was bought at such an enormous cost that the new government faced an economic crisis in 1945. Economic and financial worries not only absorbed much of the energy of ministers but threatened their whole programme of reform. It is sometimes said that Labour's welfare plans, based on a universal insurance scheme, were self-financing, involving merely a redistribution of wealth within British society. But this is not wholly true. Family allowances, for instance, were to be paid as a universal right, regardless of insurance contributions, and similarly old age pensions were to be paid in full immediately, against Beveridge's advice. Furthermore, a National Health Service was to be financed primarily from taxation and nationalisation proposals would involve the compensation of previous owners. Intractable economic realities might therefore prevent Labour from constructing even the foundations of the New Jerusalem.

The war had caused tremendous physical damage. Fewer Britons had perished than in the First World War (400,000 as opposed to 750,000), but in every other way the scale of destruction was much more significant in 1939–45. As many as half a million houses may have been destroyed, while millions of houses, factories, shops and warehouses were in a state of poor repair. In addition, almost a third of Britain's prewar shipping tonnage had not been replaced after wartime losses. But even these figures do not tell the whole story. Problems were compounded by the tremendous financial cost of the war. The basic rate of income tax had been raised to 50 per cent, while compulsory savings schemes were inaugurated, but even so Britain had to sell off foreign investments to the tune of £1,000 million – so that never again could 'invisibles' compensate for large deficits on visible trade – and to run up debts amounting to £3,500 million, compared with less than £500 million back in 1939. Indeed in 1945 Britain had the largest external debt in history. About 15 per cent of Britain's wealth had been lost in the First World War; and now the Second drained another 30 per cent. In the words of Maynard Keynes, Britain had thrown 'good housekeeping to the winds'.

From one point of view, Britain's war effort had been prodigiously successful. A far higher proportion of the country's national resources was mobilised for war than elsewhere. Unemployment disappeared, and nearly 50 per cent of a workforce expanded by the conscription of women were either in the armed forces or producing munitions. Towards the end of the war over 5 million Britons were in the armed services, while another 4 million were supplying them. But the problems of returning to a peacetime economy were correspondingly great. In 1945 only 2 per cent of Britain's workers were manufacturing for export. Not only had overseas markets been lost, resulting in a balance of payments deficit of huge proportions, but the curtailment of imports and of civilian production had created a regime of austerity and rationing which the public, naturally enough, wished to end with the cessation of hostilities. To make matters worse, the immediate postwar period saw acute worldwide shortages of raw materials, food and capital goods.

In August 1945 Keynes informed the new government that the country faced a 'financial Dunkirk', a dramatic phrase implying the likelihood of catastrophe. Overseas financial expenditure would, in his opinion, have to be drastically cut, and even then Britain would be 'virtually bankrupt and the economic basis for the hopes of the public non-existent' unless the American Lend-Lease programme of aid were continued. A few days later President Truman abruptly terminated Lend-Lease and handed Britain a bill of $650 million for goods in the pipeline. The country no longer faced war, wrote the Chancellor of the Exchequer, 'only total economic ruin'.

Britain's debts were enormous, but the huge balance of payments deficit meant that, as first priority, the government had to beg or borrow still more. Labour called upon Keynes to plead its cause; and they could have found no one more skilled. Believing that Britain, which had entered the war so much earlier than the Americans, had a moral case for a retrospective redivision of its costs, he hoped to secure a $5,000 million free gift from the Americans or, failing this, an interest-free loan. But he was able to obtain neither. By November he had to accept a loan of $3,750 million, to be repaid at 2 per cent interest from 1951. This was less than the cabinet wanted, but it was on better than commercial terms and was certainly all the Americans were willing to offer. There were also strings attached – especially the insistence that the pound should be made convertible into dollars in 1947. One Conservative MP compared the agreement to Chamberlain's act of appeasement at Munich, and *The Economist* grumbled that Britain's 'reward for losing a quarter of our national wealth in the common cause is to pay tribute for half a century to those who have been enriched by the war'. The convertibility clause has even been called a 'time bomb'. But the cabinet felt it had to acquiesce. The Chancellor judged that, without the loan, welfare reforms would have to be scrapped and that Labour's defeat at the next election would be a certainty.

At least an immediate crisis had been avoided. Labour had bought time to put the country's financial house in order and in particular to remedy the balance of payments deficit, which was especially large with the USA. The long-term economic health of the country depended on returning trade to balance. Britain therefore had to export more, particularly to North America, while keeping imports – especially American imports – as low as possible. But this was no easy task. Indeed in 1945 the value of American goods imported into Britain exceeded the cost of British exports to the USA by ten times. The American economy had boomed during the war, so that at its close the USA was in fact virtually the only large-scale supplier of goods, and the whole world wished to export to the lucrative dollar market. The experts estimated that Britain's current account deficit would continue for several years and that exports had therefore to be raised as quickly as possibly to 175 per cent of their pre-war total.

Labour was thus faced with extremely difficult economic tasks. How well did the government cope? Any answer to this question must make clear the severity of continuing problems after 1945. New crises erupted in 1947, dubbed by Hugh Dalton the 'annus horrendus'. In the early months of the year Britain suffered one of the worst winters on record. February 1947 saw the longest period without sunshine in recorded history, while temperatures were the lowest for over 100 years. The whole of the United Kingdom was covered with snow from the end of January until the middle of March. One historian has called this 'a unique aggregation of climatic malevolence'. When the thaw began, in the wettest March on record, 32 counties experienced serious flooding.

The economic effects of the weather were devastating. About 90 per cent of Britain's industrial and domestic energy was derived from coal, and the disruption of road, rail and sea traffic meant that stockpiles at the collieries could not reach the power stations. Industry soon ground to a halt, while domestic electricity was restricted for five hours a day. Industrial production fell by 50 per cent in February, and unemployment surged from 400,000 in January to around 2.5 million at the end of February.

The weather was an act of God; but the 'inactivity of Emanuel' was also an important factor. The fuel crisis had been predicted and could, with adequate preparation, have been at least mitigated by the Minister of Fuel and Power, Emanuel Shinwell. Not that he was responsible for the long-term decline of the coal industry. The pits had been performing badly throughout the interwar years and output fell in every year of the Second World War. Coal supplies had barely been adequate in the winter of 1945–6. Shinwell's remedy was nationalisation, operative from 1 January 1947. The optimistic minister believed that the psychological impact of public ownership would revitalise the miners and overcome the projected shortfall between output and national requirements. Hence not enough was done to recruit more miners – and Shinwell has been quoted as saying that Polish immigrants would enter the pits over his dead body – or to restrict the consumption of fuel before the coldest months of the year. Coal and electricity supplies were beginning to break down at the start of January 1947, even before the weather became particularly bad. Had Shinwell taken the advice of colleagues and made realistic preparations, the effects of the weather would not have been so devastating. Dalton's view, that 'the root cause of all this trouble is the insufficient stocks with which we started the winter', has been largely endorsed by historians, most notably by the recent work of Alex Robertson.

Once the crisis erupted, the government handled it well, minimising its effects. But even so, its consequences were profound. The cost to exports alone was estimated at a minimum of £100 million, and the true figure may be nearer £200 million. The export drive, on which the whole British economy hinged, may have been set back by nine months. In addition, over 20 per cent of the nation's sheep were lost, together with 50,000 cattle, while 116,000 acres of winter grain were destroyed by frost or flood. The number of people who died as a result of the winter and of fuel shortages cannot be calculated, but mortality rates were about 18 per cent higher in the first three months of 1947 than in the corresponding period the previous year. Hypothermia took a much higher toll than usual.

The climatic disasters of winter gave way to the financial horrors of the summer of 1947. It has been said that no peacetime government in modern British history faced a more daunting set of circumstances than Labour at this time. On 15 July sterling was made convertible, resulting in a run on the pound. Those with sterling assets rushed to change them into dollars; British reserves became dangerously depleted; and bankruptcy loomed menacingly close. The situation bore an uncomfortable resemblance to the 1931 crisis which had broken the second Labour government. There was even talk of a coalition. So severe were the financial problems that Treasury officials even drew up contingency plans for a 'famine food programme', in which the government would have to direct men onto the land and control the allocation of resources. Dalton feared mass unemployment, mass starvation and 'the end of our Socialist experiment, and of all our dreams!' King George VI wrote to his wife that never 'in the whole history of mankind' had things looked gloomier. The American loan was already being spent much faster than anticipated, due to rapidly increasing US export prices: now it evaporated even more rapidly. On 20 August an emergency session of the cabinet decided to go back on its agreement with the Americans and suspend convertibility, a decision felt by Dalton, who was on the verge, or perhaps in the middle, of a nervous breakdown, as a 'personal humiliation'.

The root cause of the financial crisis was probably the general state of the British economy, and in particular the trade deficit ('dollar gap') with the USA: convertibility had merely emphasised British vulnerability. Dalton bemoaned the fact that, as late as April 1947, the sum total of British exports to the States barely exceeded in value British consumption of American tobacco, with a consequent drain on reserves. It was, he said dramatically, like watching a child bleed to death. He had found no answer to the problem, but he could not be equally passive after the suspension of convertibility. Clearly the reintroduction of exchange controls would not by itself solve the problem. Britain had to make a supreme effort to cut imports and raise exports – to produce its way out of trouble by channelling new production into the export market.

The government survived the summer of 1947, but with confidence diminished. Gallup polls in August showed a Conservative lead for the first time since 1942, and in November Labour fared badly in the local elections. While economic historians have tended to praise Labour's resolute and determined policies during the latter years of the government, most political historians have seen the convertibility crisis as the key turning point in Labour's fortunes. Never, wrote Dalton, quoting Browning, was it glad confident morning again. Certainly ministers were never as optimistic or united. Attlee's performance during the crisis, Dalton wrote in his diary, had been 'catastrophic', and for a time it had seemed that the Prime Minister would be replaced. Yet it was Dalton who resigned, after a budget leak, though not before taking important but unpopular action. In his last budget, in November 1947, he increased taxation, cut government spending and imposed limits on food imports, necessitating more stringent rationing. The government was beginning to turn from the use of the physical controls inherited from the war to Keynesian demand management. A reduction in domestic demand, such as this budget would engineer, would, it was calculated, channel a greater proportion of Gross National Product into exports.

The basic effect of this policy was domestic austerity, identified especially with Dalton's successor at the Treasury, Stafford Cripps. Cripps insisted that the first national priority should be the needs of industry; second came the necessity for further capital investments; and a lowly third came the 'consumption requirements' of the people. If workers worked hard and were particularly successful, he judged, they should be given medals rather than higher wages which would only be squandered on inessentials. Hence the wartime regime of queues and shortages was intensified. It was calculated at the end of 1947 that the average British woman spent at least one hour of every day in a queue. Both bread and potatoes were rationed for the first time, by Minister of Food John Strachey ('Starve with Strachey and Shiver with Shinwell' complained the Conservatives), and the public were urged to eat such exotic items as whalemeat steaks, reindeer cutlets and the South African fish snoek (as inedible as it was unpronounceable), soon sold off as cat food.

This was certainly the 'age of austerity', necessarily so, since one man's austerity made possible another man's decent standard of living. Nevertheless, it is important to recognise that the period was not all drabness and depression. Half a million people, along with their ration books, went to Billy Butlin's holiday camps each year. Sport underwent a great revival, especially when the test matches resumed in 1946, and it was said that at the sight of Denis Compton in full flow 'the strain of long years of anxiety and affliction passed from all hearts'. (Compton made no fewer than 3,816 runs in 1947, including 18 centuries.) The average attendance at football grounds was higher in the late 1940s than ever before or since. Betting also flourished, and in 1947 alone almost £800 million were gambled. It was the heyday of the cinema as well, 1946 marking the all-time attendance record with the sale of 1,635 million tickets. In addition, the Arts Council was formed after the war and classical music flourished, as did the London theatre.

Under Cripps there was a sustained export drive and also an attempt to develop and exploit the resources of Britain's colonial empire. The Chancellor called in November 1947 for 'the tempo of African economic development' to be increased out of all recognition. In this way Britain would not only save dollar imports but be able to sell more in the dollar market. The showpiece of colonial development was 'Operation Groundnuts', the attempt to grow groundnuts in over 3 million acres of bush land in Tanganyika. In this way, it was hoped, Britain would have a valuable oil-rich food to sell at a time of world shortage of fats and oils. But in fact few nuts were ever grown and about £30 million were wasted, a failure that the Tories insisted was a national scandal. The whole project had been rushed, so that there was no pilot scheme, and generally mismanaged. Too little was known about the soil and rainfall of the land to be developed, too few trained personnel were available and there was a severe shortage of capital goods. The attempt to convert Sherman tanks into tractors – the modern equivalent of beating swords into ploughshares – may have been a noble enterprise, but it did not make for efficient agriculture. If the scheme was to work, expensive machinery would have to be bought from the USA. In other words, a venture designed to save dollars would in fact cost dollars. In 1951, unable to solve this conundrum, the government virtually abandoned the project. The attempt to solve Britain's economic ills by exploiting Africa was abandoned.

Britain's financial position was helped significantly by Marshall Aid from 1948. The Americans had been deaf to Keynes's advice in 1945 that free grants would, in the end, rebound to US advantage, but in June 1947 Secretary of State George Marshall mooted, even if rather tentatively, the US administration's willingness to make such grants. Perhaps he realised he was launching a vital aid programme, but it was Ernest Bevin, who had not been officially alerted of his speech, who then seized the initiative and helped form the Organisation for European Economic Co-operation, through which aid was co-ordinated. Britain received almost $3,000 million out of a total amount of $12,000 million, more than any other recipient. The Board of Trade calculated that without this aid rations would have been cut by a third, cotton goods would have disappeared from the market, shortages of timber would have slashed the house-building programme and unemployment would have risen steeply. No wonder Bevin described Marshall Aid as 'a lifeline to sinking men'. Recently, however, it has been argued that this aid, rather than being the 'fuel', was no more than a high-grade 'lubricant' of Europe's industrial recovery. The debate on this issue is likely to continue, as is that on US motives. Probably the programme stemmed more from American enlightened self-interest than altruism. Europeans were desperate for American dollars and without them would soon experience a depression that would not be confined to their own continent. American producers needed the European consumers that Marshall Aid guaranteed. At the same time the US government decided that a prosperous Western Europe was ultimately the most effective barrier to the spread of Communism.

Marshall Aid did not solve Britain's problems; it merely provided a breathing-space in which the British economy had to start paying its way. Nor did it prevent another financial crisis erupting in 1949, resulting in the devaluation of sterling by 30 per cent on 18 September 1949. Britain's trade with the USA was still in deficit, and signs of an American depression, which would exacerbate the problem by reducing British exports, led to a debate as to whether the pound's relationship to the dollar should be adjusted. The government dithered, its hesitations reminding the aged Lord Addison of the 1931 crisis and fuelling dangerous speculation against the pound. Again British reserves fell alarmingly, by 30 per cent between March and September 1949. The Chancellor, Stafford Cripps, set his face against devaluation, but in the end the decision was taken to reduce the value of sterling from $4.03 to $2.80, where it stayed until 1967.

Regarded at the time as a defeat for the government, in retrospect devaluation has seemed to most economic historians eminently sensible. The growth of the US economy since prewar days necessitated some currency readjustment – not so much the devaluation of the pound as the revaluation of the dollar. Since most other currencies followed Britain's example, this is in effect what happened. Indeed, the main criticism of the government is that it delayed devaluation beyond the point of maximum advantage. Devaluation would have made no sense before demobilisation had been achieved and the British economy was operating at full power: Britain would not have been producing enough to benefit from more competitive export prices, while higher import prices would have harmed the balance of payments. But by 1948–9 this was no longer the case. However, ministers were hard to convince, almost automatically regarding devaluation as an evil to be avoided. Younger ministers like Gaitskell and Wilson were converted first, but perhaps the figure who should take most credit was a civil servant, Robert Hall. Henceforth the new exchange rate made it relatively easier for British goods to sell in dollar markets. The Chancellor was able to announce at the end of 1950 that Britain would no longer need to call upon Marshall Aid: the supply was ended fifteen months ahead of schedule. But there was no boom. The final months of Labour administration were economically scarred by the Korean war. Some said defence spending, and overseas commitments generally, were already too great for Britain's economy to bear. Now Labour decided to increase spending dramatically, to a total of £4,700 million in 1951–4 (around 14 per cent of total national income), which turned out to be more than could be spent. With a third world war a real prospect, it was no time for 'good housekeeping'. The result was a reduction in welfare provision and the resignation of Bevan. Furthermore the war led to a decisive movement in the terms of trade against Britain. A steep rise in import prices had deleterious effects not only on the balance of payments but also on inflation.

At first sight Labour's economic record seems poor. Problems were inevitable, but its handling of each issue showed palpable weaknesses. It failed to take adequate precautions to prevent the fuel crisis during the early months of 1947 and the convertibility crisis of July and August 1947. Ministers dithered over devaluation, and they devoted too much money to defence in 1951. All these criticisms are generally accepted by economic historians. Alec Cairncross, for instance, has written that on one issue after another ministers were slow to grasp the issues at stake and had difficulty reaching sensible conclusions: they tended to be 'the reluctant pupils of their officials'. And yet those historians who have detailed Labour's misunderstandings and failures have nevertheless tended to conclude that in fact the government did a relatively good job and should be praised rather than censured for its economic management. According to Cairncross, 1945–51 were years when the government knew what it wanted and led the country purposefully. Labour ministers forged techniques of economic management which successive governments were soon to follow.

There are several reasons for a positive assessment. The most obvious is one which historians have tended to discount. Except during the winter of 1946–7, Britain experienced full employment, in sharp contrast to the interwar period when at least 10 per cent of the insured workforce were continuously out of work. Labour seemed to have achieved the aim of 'jobs for all' set out in its manifesto. Unemployment in 1948–50 averaged about 1.6 per cent, and in 1951 it stood at a mere 1.2 per cent – so low that some economists even began to talk about an 'over-full' level of employment which made it difficult to contain inflation. Yet these high employment levels seem to have stemmed largely from the simple fact that demand was high due to postwar restocking. It was a seller's market. Britain could sell all it was producing – and more – and therefore the government did not have to create jobs itself. Nevertheless, it should be remembered that had the government not tackled the balance of payments problem, the consequences for employment could have been very grim indeed. Nor should it be forgotten that the government vigorously applied the 1945 and 1950 Distribution of Industry Acts to direct jobs to the former depressed areas, so avoiding the regional contrast between prosperity and poverty which had characterised the 1930s. Finally, Labour avoided the policies which, after the First World War, ended an inflationary boom with a deflationary slump.

The traditional way of approaching the enormous problems that faced the government after 1945 would have been to reduce expenditure, raise interest rates and increase taxation – in short, to deflate the economy. But Labour turned its face against such harsh policies, which would have increased unemployment and ended expensive social reforms. Labour's cuts in public expenditure were tactical manoeuvres, and there was nothing similar to the swingeing Geddes Axe of 1922. Spending on social welfare was pruned but not slashed, and interest rates were kept deliberately low so as not to stifle investment. Labour also avoided the industrial strife which had scarred 1918–22: far fewer days were lost in industrial action after the Second World War than after the First (about 14 million in 1945–51 compared to 192 million in 1918–24). Attlee was prepared, on occasions, to use troops to break strikes, but in 1948 his government successfully urged voluntary wage restraint on the unions, and for two years this was effective. This was probably Britain's most successful postwar incomes policy, though by 1950 there were signs of growing tension, increased by the price rises that accompanied the Korean war. Even so, there was no wage-price inflationary spiral under Attlee's government. Inflation did occur, but it did not reach the heights seen elsewhere at the same time.

On the whole, despite the multifarious economic and financial problems that beset the country, the government determinedly stuck to its programmes of social reform. A less determined government might not have done so. If, for instance, the Conservatives had been elected in 1945, with a less than wholehearted commitment to social reform, they would have had at the very least an ideal excuse to postpone reforming legislation. Churchill refused to commit his wartime government to implementing the Beveridge report because he thought that, after the war, Britain would not be able to afford it: he might well have decided, in the circumstances of 1945–7, that he had been right. Labour, on the other hand, resolutely paid the price for their reforms – the continuance of austerity for longer than the British public wished. Crippsian policies were electorally unpopular, but they were economically beneficial, so that the 'age of austerity' made possible the subsequent 'age of affluence' in the 1950s. Conservative governments were able to reap the benefits of Labour's achievement and to preside over a period when economic problems were far less fearsome than in 1945–51.

The true measure of Labour's achievement can be shown statistically. In 1946–51 industrial production increased by a third, Britain enjoying one of the longest periods of economic growth in the postwar period. Growth as high as 4 per cent was achieved in 1948, 1949 and 1950. Indeed, in 1950 productivity in British industry was at an all-time high and had increased faster in Britain than in the United States. The wartime slogan 'Britain can take it' had been transformed into 'Britain can make it'. The balance of payments was the key problem, and here there was considerable success. Exports rose significantly faster than imports – exports grew in 1945–50 by 77 per cent, while imports grew by only 15 per cent – and by 1948 there was a trade balance, earlier than even the optimists had expected. A surplus existed in 1948–50, though the unfavourable terms of trade associated with the Korean war caused temporary problems in 1951. Britain's share of world exports grew from 17.5 per cent before the war to 20.7 per cent in 1950. A balance of trade with the dollar area was not achieved, but the gap did close significantly and ceased to be regarded as the insoluble problem it had once seemed. Balance came about in 1953. In short, it was a reasonably good record and it could have been much worse. Most other postwar governments have failed to do as well.

Yet Labour does not deserve the whole credit for Britain's economic performance, and it is often said that it indulged much more in rhetoric about planning than in actual physical actions. The export drive was due to other factors, as well as the efforts of the Board of Trade and the determination of the government to inhibit domestic consumption. Labour was also, to some

5

Labour's achievements: domestic affairs

The Labour administration of 1945 was the first government in British history to be elected on a clear programme of reforms specified in its manifesto. (It was also the first – and perhaps the last – government to succeed in implementing the promises that it had made.) Financial and economic conditions were inauspicious, but Labour was in no mood to be deterred by circumstances. Dalton recalled that in 1945 'There was exhilaration among us, joy and hope, determination and confidence. We felt exalted, dedicated, walking on air, walking with destiny.' Bliss was it then to be alive, but to be a socialist was very heaven. Britain might no longer be the dominant economic power in the world, but even so it was the exemplar for mankind. 'If we fail,' wrote Gordon Walker, 'democracy fails in Britain. And that means in the world.' The result was an unprecedented flurry of legislative activity. In the first parliamentary session no fewer than 75 measures were enacted, and in total the parliament elected in 1945 passed 347 separate Acts. There was, in Hennessy's phrase, 'a parliamentary production line' of bills under Labour.

Social services

It is sometimes said that Attlee's Labour governments constructed the 'welfare state' (a term that became popular as Britain's constructive alternative to Hitler's 'warfare state'). In fact Labour's achievement was more one of modernising, improving and greatly extending an existing structure than of building an entirely new edifice. Much of the groundwork had been done before the First World War, especially by Lloyd George. In 1908 he had introduced old age pensions, and in 1911 a system of unemployment and health insurance. The interwar period saw a significant, if piecemeal and haphazard, extension of these schemes. By 1925 old age pensions were paid as a matter of right to insured workers and their wives at the age of 65 and, on a non-contributory basis, to those aged 70 and over whose incomes fell below prescribed levels. Compulsory health insurance was also extended, so that by 1939 it covered almost 20 million workers, over half Britain's working population. But their dependants were not covered, and neither were the self-employed; and no dental or ophthalmic treatment was included, only the services of a general practitioner. Hospital treatment was available, at a cost, from about 1,000 voluntary hospitals, which were dependent on private subscriptions and charitable donations, and about 2,000 municipal hospitals. But the standard of hospital provision, and of medical care generally, varied enormously from one part of the country to another. Unemployment insurance was also extended between the wars: it covered larger numbers of workers and provided both allowances for dependants and also 'uncovenanted benefit' (the dole) to cover workers whose insurance cover had expired, though only after a hotly resented means test on the whole household. Indeed, by 1939 no fewer than eighteen separate means tests were administered by seven separate government departments. Social services were clearly a mosaic – or perhaps a crazy paving – of provisions, rather than a unified, efficient system. Furthermore, there were obvious and glaring anomalies. The system of workmen's compensation was clearly inadequate; and a man out of work through unemployment could claim allowances for dependants which those idle through illness could not. In many ways it was an administrative nightmare.

The war years saw some changes. In particular the Emergency Hospital Service was set up. Nazi bombs fell impartially on the insured and the uninsured alike, and so the government arranged that all hospitals should set aside beds for war casualties. Above all, the war saw an important rise in the public's expectations. The idea of a better postwar world, symbolised by the Beveridge report, became one of the aims for which people believed they were fighting.

Beveridge, who had a tremendous talent for self-publicity, wrote eye-catchingly that a 'revolutionary moment in the world's history is a time for revolutions, not for patching'. Nevertheless, his report was in some ways an example of patching, even if of an ingenious kind, together with tidy-minded and sensible bureaucratic rationalisation. He decided that all benefits should be administered by one new ministry. Similarly all contributions (for health, unemployment, accidents, pensions, etc.) should be unified into one standard weekly payment. In this way a more efficient administrative structure would be provided. The essential novelty was that his scheme was to be universal: everyone could take out additional, private insurance, but only in addition to, not instead of, the state provision. Hence all would be entitled to state benefits as of right, thus avoiding the need for a means test. Furthermore, Beveridge insisted that, in order to eliminate poverty, this insurance scheme should be accompanied by 'children's allowances', the setting up of a free national health service and the maintenance of full employment.

Labour's social achievements admittedly owed much to wartime planning in general and Beveridge's ideas in particular. While it was the Labour government which first paid family (children's) allowances from 1946, it was the coalition which had passed the necessary legislation. In addition, the 1946 Industrial Injuries Act – making compensation for industrial injury a social service rather than the responsibility of individual employers – differed in only small ways from legislation planned by the previous government. Most important of all, the National Insurance Act of 1946 derived directly from Beveridge's inspiration. Under this Act a universal scheme of compulsory flat-rate contributions and of flat-rate benefits was administered from a new Ministry of National Insurance based in Newcastle, with local offices throughout the country. The insurance fund paid out benefits to those who were unemployed or ill, as well as maternity and death grants, old age pensions for women at 60 and men at 65 and widows' pensions. Similarly Labour's National Assistance Act of 1948 – whereby those who did not qualify for insurance benefits, falling through the safety net erected from the cradle to the grave, could claim means-tested benefits – was implicit in the Beveridge report.

47

Yet those, like Paul Addison, who claim that Beveridge provided an actual 'blueprint' for the postwar welfare state, surely exaggerate. They ignore the fact that at its conference in 1942, before the publication of the Beveridge report, Labour had itself endorsed a comprehensive scheme of social security. Second, they play down the significant differences that existed between Labour's scheme and Beveridge's advice. Pensions, for instance, were to be paid in full and immediately, rather than after a period of time in which those to become eligible to collect pensions would be paying contributions. Furthermore, many of Beveridge's ideas – on the need for a national health service, for instance – were general assumptions rather than precise policy blueprints. As Labour's Minister of Health from 1945, Aneurin Bevan drew up plans for a comprehensive health service virtually from scratch.

Various proposals existed at the end of the war for a new national health service. Bevan swept them aside as inadequate. He realised that the previous system had to be extended to cover the whole population and that it had now to encompass hospital treatment. But if the whole population was to be covered while only adult workers were paying insurance contributions, the insurance basis of the previous system could no longer be expected to survive. In addition, a way had to be found to produce equal medical care throughout the country. How to achieve these desirable ends was an exceedingly complicated matter.

Under the new dispensation the bulk of NHS finances would have to come from general taxation, though a small proportion might come from the National Insurance Fund. Bevan decided to keep the basis of the old system, in that each general practitioner would have a 'panel' of patients, but the remuneration of the doctors would change. As under the old system, doctors would be paid a capitation fee for each patient on their panels, but now they would have a small annual salary as well – vital, Bevan thought, for young GPs trying to build up their practices. In addition, the buying and selling of practices was to be abolished, the GPs who had already bought theirs being compensated by the state (to a total of £66 million). Doctors could also be forbidden by a professional committee from practising in 'over-doctored' areas and encouraged by financial incentives to settle in areas with shortages. Members of the public could choose which GP they signed on with, and the doctors too would have a choice. GPs were not forced to work for the NHS: they could confine themselves to private patients or retain private in addition to NHS patients. Dental and ophthalmic services would also come under the system.

Perhaps Bevan's most creative decision was that all hospitals should be nationalised, an issue which led to cabinet rows with Morrison, who wanted to keep municipal hospitals under local authority jurisdiction. Bevan reasoned that only a unified system of hospitals could hope to produce common standards of health care. As with the GPs, the hospital consultants could not be forced to work in NHS hospitals, and indeed there seemed a danger that they might set up private nursing homes of their own. To reduce the possibility of this, Bevan agreed that NHS consultants could also treat private patients and that they might do so in 'pay beds' in the state's hospitals.

As Michael Foot has shown with a wealth of detail, Bevan's scheme met tremendously stubborn resistance from the British Medical Association, the professional body of GPs. There were fears that Bevan would interfere with clinical freedom and that doctors were being transformed into civil servants. GPs voted by large majorities against the minister's main provisions. The NHS bill became law in November 1946 but the service was not due to come into operation until July 1948, and for a long time it looked likely to be stillborn. In February 1948 the GPs voted eight to one against joining the scheme. Members of the BMA even described Bevan as Britain's equivalent to Adolf Hitler and the proposed NHS as a form of national socialism. In fact, Bevan showed a constructive ability to compromise and to assuage the fears of the doctors. In particular he insisted that if, after three years, the GPs were not satisfied with their payment of capitation fees plus salary, they could be paid by fees alone. Soon the GPs rejected the implacable opposition of the leaders of the BMA and joined the new service.

In some ways, as John Campbell has argued, Bevan was fortunate that the BMA opposed him. Their opposition convinced Labour supporters that the NHS was a radical scheme and distracted attention from the compromises which, as a socialist, Bevan had been reluctant to grant. Disliking market-place medicine, the minister wanted to ensure that poverty was no disadvantage, and wealth no advantage, to good health

49

care. He therefore particularly disliked the existence of 'pay beds' in NHS hospitals. Private medicine within the NHS could not be defended on grounds of principle; but such a compromise had been needed to secure the participation of the specialists. Bevan hoped that, in time, the NHS would work so well that private medicine would wither away. Certainly it was immediately popular, and there was a tremendous call for its services. In the first year of the NHS 18,000 GPs wrote 187,000 prescriptions, 8.5 million dental patients were treated and 5.25 million pairs of spectacles were dispensed, while another 3 million were on order.

In consequence, the Service in its first year cost about £250 million, twice the amount originally estimated. Soon Bevan was submitting supplementary estimates, while his colleagues were being asked to make cuts. In 1950–1 the bill was around £350 million, and in 1951 charges for false teeth and spectacles were imposed, resulting in Bevan's resignation. Colleagues felt that Bevan had become obsessed with his 'precious health service'. But very few would today deny that the NHS was probably Labour's greatest achievement, much of the credit for which must go to Bevan. Without him a national health service almost certainly would have been set up, but not the one which was inaugurated in 1948. Historians have speculated that perhaps a service might have been set up in stages rather than all at once. Nor, in retrospect, does its early expenditure seem unduly high. There was such a legacy of health problems to be overcome that the initial costs were bound to be high, but by 1950–1 spending was evening out and was not out of control. The Guillebaud Report of 1956 established that in 1949–54 the cost of the NHS fell as a proportion of gross national product, and those historians – and in particular Correlli Barnett – who see significant causal connections between increased welfare spending and British decline have failed to explain how Britain's successful economic competitors managed to spend more on social services. Perhaps the real charge to be made is a social rather than an economic one, not that too much but that too little was spent on health care. For instance, not a single new hospital was built during the first seven years of the NHS. An official survey of 1961 referred to 'hospitals which should have been blown up, slum property, appalling fire risks . . . [and] degrading conditions for patients and staff'. There were also important unsolved organisational problems besetting the Service.

Bevan was also the minister in charge of housing. In this sphere he was less successful and for a time was considered a definite failure. Opinion polls showed that housing was the most important single priority for the electorate, but by 1949 twice as many people were dissatisfied as satisfied with the government's housing record. Bevan's task was certainly enormous. About half a million houses had been destroyed or made uninhabitable during the war and as many as one third of all houses in Britain were in need of serious repair. Added to this, the immediate postwar years saw an unprecedented number of marriages and births. Never had more people been seeking houses, and never had there been greater competition for building materials that were in acutely short supply. Perhaps a separate Ministry of Housing should have been created. The joke was that Bevan was able to keep only 'half a nye' on housing. Progress at first was slow, and in 1946 homeless squatters seized unused army camps. But, in the end, much was achieved. Bevan channelled government subsidies through local authorities and insisted that only one privately built house could be erected for every four council houses, in order to direct limited resources to those most in need. In addition he ensured that new council houses were of a good standard and size (at least 1,000 square feet, compared with a prewar average of 800), drawing forth from Dalton the comment that Bevan was 'a tremendous Tory'. Perhaps George VI was nearer the truth when he judged that Bevan wanted real homes and not merely 'boxes of bricks'. The minister insisted that he would not be responsible for creating a country of East Ends and West Ends, and indeed he hoped that publicly provided housing would soon prove attractive to all classes in society. To his mind, council houses would be of better quality than private houses built by speculative builders out for a quick profit.

By 1951 several hundred thousand dwellings had been repaired or converted and 160,000 prefabricated houses had been constructed. Most important of all, just over one million new houses had been built. This was not as many as were needed, and no doubt more could have been built if standards had been lower, but it was a significant achievement none the less. Indeed, Bevan's scheme would have produced more houses but for government cutbacks, following the 1947 convertibility crisis.

In education, Labour was primarily concerned with implementing wartime plans, specifically Butler's 1944 Education Act. This is not to say that the existence of Labour ministers made no difference in this important field. Despite the parlous economic and financial conditions of 1947, for instance, Labour raised the school-leaving age to 15 in April. Ellen Wilkinson had to battle fiercely in cabinet to achieve this, and the Conservatives might well have postponed it longer. But on the whole Labour devoted its energies more to the practicalities of providing schools and teachers than to broad educational philosophy. 'Prefab' classrooms were hastily built, and the Emergency Training Scheme, of one rather than the customary two years' duration, turned out an extra 25,000 teachers in 1945–51. The educational system thereby coped with the extra places demanded by the raising of the leaving age.

Teachers were given a pretty free hand with the content of their teaching, and the new tripartite division of schools – into grammar, technical and modern schools – went largely unchallenged. Only as it left office did Labour commit itself to the more egalitarian comprehensive system. Nor did Labour reform the system of public schools, which some had hoped and others feared would actually be abolished. The government tried to implement the 1944 Fleming report, which argued that 25 per cent of public school places should be reserved for children with local authority scholarships, but local councils naturally enough preferred to spend on their own schools. Paradoxically, a period of 'socialist' administration proved the heyday of the public school system.

By 1951, despite the introduction of some health service charges, Labour was seen pre-eminently as the party of the welfare state. It deserved this reputation. Despite adverse circumstances the Labour governments had struggled to give effect to reforms for which the Beveridge report and other wartime plans were only a partial guide. Yet they were criticised by their own left wing, and by some later historians, for basing state benefits on an insurance scheme which, in effect, amounted to an unfair poll tax that preserved inequalities. Instead, according to this school of thought, the costs of the welfare state should have been derived solely from direct, graduated taxation – a scheme which would have tended to redistribute wealth within British society. Critics from elsewhere in the political spectrum, however, have judged that welfare spending was more lavish than the economy could afford and that funds should have been targeted to those in particular need.

The effects of Labour's reforms have also been hard to quantify. The party chairman claimed at the 1950 annual conference that 'Poverty has been abolished, hunger is unknown. The sick are tended. The old folks are cherished, our children are growing up in a land of plenty.' Rowntree's 1951 survey of the standard of living in York (with only 2.8 per cent below the poverty line) showed remarkable improvements on that for 1936 (with 31.1 per cent falling below), and all the evidence shows that in the nation as a whole standards of health were rising. On the other hand, despite the insurance provisions, an uncomfortably large number received means-tested benefits under the 1948 National Assistance Act. Research from the late 1950s onwards shows that poverty undoubtedly still existed in Britain and made Rowntree's conclusions seem unduly optimistic. Perhaps the key point is that though Labour's reforms provided a wide range of benefits, the level at which they were paid – a crucial issue – was, in real terms, generally below that prescribed by Beveridge in 1942. Benefits were not index-linked and therefore could not possibly eliminate poverty at a time of inflation. Claimants would receive not subsistence allowances but what the government of the day decided the country could afford. Perhaps a country dependent on US aid could have done no more, and supporters of the government would argue that the alternative to what was achieved was no achievement at all. Yet critics point out that though Labour was spending far higher sums on social services than, for instance, in the interwar years, the proportion of overall government revenue devoted to this area (46.1 per cent in 1950) was not so very different from that in the mid-1930s.

Nationalisation

Labour's commitment to the common ownership of the means of production had given the party a distinctive political position ever since 1918, and in 1945 this was the principle which most distinguished the party from Conservatives and Liberals. But, despite Clause IV and regardless of a vote at the 1944 Labour conference in favour of a very extensive programme of national-isation, Labour did not intend to take the whole of British industry into public ownership. In its 1945 manifesto the party pledged itself to nationalise the Bank of England, the coal industry, gas and electricity, inland transport and iron and steel. In addition, it would 'work towards' land nationalisation. There was also a reference to industries 'not yet ripe for public ownership'; but which precise industries were meant, and when or indeed whether they would be nationalised, was left open, presumably for future parliaments to decide.

Many socialists believed that, on grounds of principle, the state should control at least the 'basic' industries. But Labour's proposals were justified to the electorate in 1945 simply on grounds of efficiency. A Labour government would aim to create a prosperous economy with full employment, and nationalisation was presented as a means to this end. Each industry was to have applied to it 'the test of national service': if it was serving the nation, well and good; but if it was inefficient, then the government would have to step in. The coal industry, which had been 'floundering chaotically' for decades, was overripe for nationalisation. Gas was clearly an ailing industry by the end of the war; and, while the *generation* of electricity had been in public hands since 1926, private *suppliers* had failed to standardise voltages and currents. The public ownership of gas and electricity was therefore expected to lead to lower charges and better research and development. Similarly, only public ownership could hope to produce a properly unified transport system. As for iron and steel – included in the manifesto as a concession to the 1944 conference – Labour insisted that the substitution of public ownership for private monopoly would lead to new efficiency and consequently lower prices.

There seemed nothing doctrinaire or threatening about this programme. Moreover, Labour characteristically pledged itself to provide fair compensation for existing owners and to promote good conditions and 'proper status' for the men and women who worked in these industries. Clearly Labour accepted a 'mixed economy' with both public and private sectors. Debate would soon focus on the balance between the two; but in the parliament elected in 1945, the government would have its hands full in bringing the industries specified in its manifesto into the public domain.

The new government lost no time in implementing its pledges. Nationalisation of the Bank of England was first on the agenda.

In the past Labour had contemplated nationalising all the banks, but its more hopeful theoreticians now believed that control of the Bank of England would spread government influence throughout the banking system. In fact the Treasury and the Bank already worked closely together, and so in practice little changed. Dalton expressed this truth metaphorically: 'the Old Man of the Treasury and the Old Lady of Threadneedle Street', who had for some time been living in sin, were now to be married. Nationalisation therefore to a large extent merely formalised an existing arrangement. Coal nationalisation was scarcely more controversial. Everyone recognised that only thorough changes could possibly revive this ailing industry. Churchill told the Commons that his party accepted the principle of nationalisation, provided that adequate compensation was paid. It was. A tribunal decided that the 850 owners should be compensated with £164 million – a figure they accepted as reasonable, which probably meant that it was generous. In fact Labour paid a total of around £2,700 million in compensation for its whole nationalisation programme.

The nationalisation of civil aviation was also relatively uncontroversial, even though it had not been included in the manifesto. The new legislation built on wartime coalition plans: Labour established British European Airways and British South American Airways to complement the already existing British Overseas Airways Corporation. The Cable and Wireless Act, the last act of nationalisation in 1946, attracted scarcely any notice: the government bought out the stock of a company operating telecommunication links within the Commonwealth in which it already had a minority holding. The Transport Bill, by which the government acquired 52,000 miles of railway track, 2,000 miles of canals and 450,000 road haulage vehicles, was more contentious. Most people accepted the need to nationalise the railways but road haulage was more problematic. Local bus services were exempt, but Labour wished to take control of all long-distance road haulage, on the grounds that only then could competition with the railways be eliminated and a co-ordinated transport system be achieved. But after extensive debates in parliament it was decided that there should be no control of local operators covering less than 40 miles or of hauliers who only carried their own goods. Partly as a result, the 1947 Transport Act, in the words of William Ashworth, was 'not so much the triumphant inauguration of a definitive era of an integrated public service . . . as the start of a long and painful series of designs, redesigns, dismantling, reorganisations, and further reorganisations'. The Electricity (1947) and Gas (1948) Acts also attracted opposition. Indeed when the Gas Bill reached the committee stage the Conservatives organised a filibuster, tabling over 800 amendments. The Commons committee sat for a mammoth continuous session of 50 hours, with an all-night buffet laid on. The Conservatives had recovered from the shock of defeat and were beginning to harass the government.

Not surprisingly, the Tories put up their most determined opposition to plans to nationalise iron and steel. Whereas they might acquiesce in the public ownership of derelict industries or public utilities, they drew the line at profitable firms. If steel were nationalised, they reasoned, where would it all stop? Would any industry be safe? Lord Salisbury insisted that the Steel Bill constituted 'a definite step towards Communism'. The surprising thing, perhaps, is that several Labour ministers opposed the scheme as well. The proposal had found a place in the 1945 manifesto only very narrowly, and Morrison had been against its inclusion. The industry was far less inefficient than, say, coal mining or the railways; nor was there any union pressure for public ownership. Did the industry really fail the 'test of national service'? Nationalisation was postponed in 1947, and the government flirted with ideas of control that stopped short of nationalisation; but in the end Dalton, Cripps, Bevin and Bevan had their way. Dalton demanded of his colleagues 'whether we were a Socialist Government or not . . . and how we could defend going back on our pledge at the Election'. He and others believed that control of such a fundamental industry as steel would help the government dominate the 'commanding heights' of the economy.

But first a new Parliament Bill had to be introduced. Under existing legislation, the House of Lords could delay bills for a maximum of two years (three sessions): if they did this with the Steel Bill, as they seemed certain to do, a new election would precede nationalisation. Hence the Labour government in 1949, as a pre-emptive measure, restricted the delaying powers of the Lords to a single year (two sessions). Even so, it was decided not to invoke the new legislation. The Lords did not in fact reject the Steel Bill: they merely amended it so that nationalisation would not become effective until after the next election. Since, by this time, another election could not be long delayed, the government acquiesced. Not surprisingly, many Labour supporters decided that the whole issue had been mistimed if not actually bungled.

By 1948–9 nationalisation was tending to become unpopular. The sugar firm Tate and Lyle, fearing a state takeover, ran an effective advertising campaign, with the cartoon character 'Mr Cube' brandishing his sword to ward off incursions from the overmighty state. Even some Labour supporters were losing interest in it. This was partly due to the form of nationalisation that had been adopted. Rather than the state running nationalised industries, as it did with the Post Office or the royal dockyards and ordnance factories, they were run by semiautonomous public corporations – the National Coal Board, the British Transport Commission, the Gas Council and so on. The power of ministers to intervene was left ill-defined and therefore uncertain (though it is now coming to be recognised that Labour ministers intervened rather more often and more forcefully than used to be assumed). Nor was any provision made for workers' representation at board level. Indeed these powerful bodies were run by people of generally capitalist outlook and conviction. For example, a former mine owner Lord Hyndley became chairman of the Coal Board, and the former Governor of the Bank of England, Lord Catto, became the new Governor. In fact it was not easy to find suitably experienced personnel to serve on the Boards, given the lack of job security and the relatively low salaries. But according to critics it was 'the negation first of all of socialism and secondly of sanity itself' to nationalise an industry and then leave it in the control of the Tories. Was this 'the best obtainable system of popular administration and control' promised by Clause IV? Certainly this form of administration tended to rob nationalisation of its maximum psychological impact: the workers in the newly nationalised industries never felt they were working for themselves, at least once the initial euphoria amongst the miners had worn off. The 'us' and 'them' attitude persisted, minimising the degree to which nationalisation promoted more harmonious industrial relations.

The historians Alan Sked and Chris Cook have dismissed Labour's whole nationalisation programme as merely 'an administrative manoeuvre'. It was public ownership without real public control. The Conservative Harold Macmillan averred that it was not socialism but 'state capitalism'. The public corporation form of nationalisation was certainly unambitious, though in fact there were few alternatives readily available.

Cripps insisted that there could be no worker control or even worker participation in management decisions because the workers did not wish it and were not ready for it. Certainly most union leaders wished to preserve traditional, adversarial wage-bargaining: trade union participation in management decisions might compromise their independence. Morrison too was perfectly happy with the public corporations: indeed he had, to a large extent, provided the model with his London Transport Executive of the 1930s. Attlee, who in 1922 had called for thorough industrial democracy, had now abandoned such radicalism; but even so he realised that something was amiss. 'In socialised industries the board is a very long way from the rank and file', he wrote to Morrison, 'yet really efficient working depends on the creation of a team spirit.' He wished to see an '*esprit de corps* of the pits', and that depended more on 'comradeship in the smaller units' than on 'exhortation from above'. He asked Morrison to look into the matter, but nothing was done. Morrison hoped that a peripatetic team of efficiency experts might examine each industry; but it was decided that the Boards would resent such interference.

By 1951 Labour's nationalisation was complete. Roughly one in ten men and women then worked for the newly nationalised industries (including 888,000 transport workers and 765,000 miners), and the public sector as a whole accounted for about 20 per cent of the British economy. To some this was far too much, for to their minds nationalisation was associated with loss-making and inefficiency. In reality, however, this perception largely reflected the kind of industries which the state had taken over – derelict industries in need of massive investment and also public service industries. Taking over the railways, for instance, was in many ways a 'rescue act', and no one believed that the mines could be run profitably. (In fact coal output rose significantly from 1946 to 1951, by which time productivity had never been higher.) At least under state control there could be the provision of decent conditions and adequate safety levels. Fatal accidents in the mines were far fewer than ever before in 1948, and fewer still in 1949. Nor would rural electrification have been carried so far under private ownership. The area electricity boards were charged to distribute electrical supplies to 'those who require them', and indeed every nationalised industry was required to take account of the 'public interest' in its activities. In addition the government encouraged the newly nationalised industries to keep prices down, with a consequent benefit to the consumer and the economy as a whole, though to the detriment of the image of nationalisation's efficiency. (It has been said that 'profit' was a dirty word to the nationalisers of 1945–51. Hence, when the National Coal Board's revenue exceeded its expenditure, this was referred to as 'excess' or 'surplus revenues' and never as profit.) Even so, Cable and Wireless made very healthy profits. A good case for the nationalised industries could have been made by 1951, but poor public relations meant that it tended to go by default.

Fundamentalists in the Labour party held fast to their creed and called for more nationalisation. Why not nationalise profitable private companies like the chemical giant ICI? Then profits would accrue to the government, and thus to the community as a whole, rather than to individuals who were already wealthy. Bevan argued that of course nationalisation was not popular: in nationalising industries the government was in effect sowing the seed of future wealth – never as immediately appealing as sharing out the fruits of previous labours. Moreover, he and others of similar mind insisted that further nationalisation would, in the end, affect power relations within society, the true socialist goal. Early examples of nationalisation, with over-generous compensation of previous owners, really had little or no effect on the distribution of wealth and power. Indeed, they may even have made the rich richer. It was also said that the government, with its emphasis on industrial efficiency, was lusting after false gods: the aim was surely not to improve the existing system but to change it.

Criticisms of the government's nationalisation measures poured in from left and right, and most historical verdicts have tended to highlight their shortcomings. It has been said that the purpose of nationalisation had never been properly clarified: industrial efficiency was its justification, but was this also its true purpose? Another common complaint is that the nationalised industries remained separate entities, so that, for instance, there was no properly integrated energy policy. Even the separate branches of the transport industry competed against each other. Pollard insists that the nationalised industries were merely 'anomalies in a private enterprise economy'. Others have echoed Macmillan's view that the nationalised industries comprised 'state capitalism' rather than socialism. Perhaps Labour was merely propping up capitalism, by channelling public funds into ailing industries, rather than providing a challenging alternative to it. To socialists, Labour had implemented its programme of public ownership, with a few additions, and yet the result was less than had been desired or expected. It must nevertheless be admitted that Labour's programme of social ownership has proved remarkably influential. After victory in 1951, the Tories only privatised steel and road haulage. They thus tacitly endorsed the bulk of Labour's programme, exposing much of their previous criticism – such as Macmillan's insistence that Labour should 'let sleeping dogmas lie' – as merely rhetoric. Both parties accepted the 'mixed economy' for several decades. Ashworth has recently judged that the nationalised industries as a whole were 'neither an inspiring success nor a hopeless failure'.

The privatisations of recent years have undone much, though not yet all, of Attlee's legislation. Will the performance of these industries under private shareholders expose the futility of the era of nationalisation or, on the contrary, emphasise the utility of state control of natural monopolies in the national interest? Time alone will enable us to answer this fascinating question.

6

Labour's achievements: external affairs

Foreign policy

Domestic issues provoked little controversy within the Labour party until the issue of steel nationalisation from 1947 onwards. Foreign affairs, however, produced more dissension in the earlier rather than the later years. Soon after the 1945 election, left-wing critics berated the Foreign Secretary, Ernest Bevin, for backing royalists in Greece and for lending British aid to Franco-Dutch attempts to regain control of their Far Eastern colonies from local nationalists. Then Anglo-Soviet friction and Britain's alignment with the USA against the USSR in the Cold War added fuel to the flames. Was this a 'socialist foreign policy'? Was this 'Left understanding Left'? One wit decided that the Foreign Secretary was really Eden grown fat. Bevin became widely regarded, in Churchill's phrase, as 'a working-class John Bull', much to the dismay of critics on the left. But left-wing criticisms then died down. Public opinion began to endorse the critical view of the Soviet Union presented in Orwell's *Animal Farm*. Soviet aggression in Prague and then the Soviet blockade of Berlin, both in 1948, convinced the party that its government's policy was broadly correct. Many historical accounts, and in particular Alan Bullock's masterly biography of Bevin, have endorsed this favourable view. Bullock is convinced that Bevin was one of Britain's best foreign secretaries: Marshall Aid and, more significantly, NATO were the monuments to his constructive genius. But some in the party, while disillusioned with Stalin, nevertheless wished Britain to lead a third force, a genuinely socialist alternative to the capitalist USA and the communist Soviet Union. Perhaps Bevin was being led astray by the Old Etonians at the Foreign Office? According to one Labour backbencher he was 'a Titan grown weary', of whom the Foreign Office took advantage to continue unchecked 'its normal routine of unplanned catastrophe', an interpretation recently endorsed by John Saville. To critical left-wing historians, Bullock's biography is little more than a very erudite and scholarly form of hero worship.

Britain's position in world affairs in 1945 was an unenviable one. It had massive prestige, having fought longest against Hitler, but massive debts to match. The British empire – 'the greatest example of strategic over-extension in history' (Liddell Hart) – was, against the odds, intact at the end of the war, and now Britain had additional policing duties in Greece, the Far East and elsewhere. Indeed, in Germany Britain found itself administering a zone which could not feed itself; and as a result British taxpayers had to pay to feed their former enemies, while managing on reduced rations themselves. The nation could ill afford such commitments. The obvious course of action was therefore twofold: to scale down commitments to match diminished resources and to settle problems peacefully by negotiation and compromise rather than confrontation and expensive preparations for war. How persistently and constructively Labour tried to achieve these aims is debatable.

At the end of the war Foreign Office officials tended to fall into the trap of regarding economic weakness as merely temporary. They therefore saw little need to disengage the country from its traditional world role. Bevin himself clung to this view. If only British colonies in Africa could be developed, he mused, 'we could have the US dependent on us, and eating out of our hand, in four or five years' – a vision of the future which may make the NATO partnership with the USA seem decidedly second-best. Whereas Attlee, supported by his economy-minded Chancellor, wanted to pull out of the Middle East in 1946, Bevin was adamant that Britain had to stay – and the three Chiefs of Staff threatened to resign if Britain did withdraw. Even Attlee, together with an inner core of ministers, decided to build the atomic bomb, a very expensive undertaking and one moreover that was concealed from the House of Commons, the initial cost of £100 million being carefully camouflaged in the financial estimates. This decision may have been strategically justified, in that Britain was within range of Soviet bombers and the USSR was itself actively developing nuclear weapons: thirty atomic bombs could, in the words of Chiefs of Staff's technical advisers, 'produce collapse in this country'. But it was also a knee-jerk reaction – what one civil servant has described as 'an "of course" decision'. Naturally Britain must have the most powerful weapons that existed. 'We've got to have this,' insisted Bevin. 'We have got to have this thing over here whatever it costs . . . . We've got to have the bloody Union Jack on top of it.'

Perhaps politicians – especially the egotistical Foreign Secretary – were suffering from delusions of grandeur: they simply could not countenance the idea that Britain was no longer the great power it had once been. In 1949 Sir Henry Tizzard, chief scientific adviser to the Ministry of Defence, complained that 'We are not a Great Power and never will be again. We are a great nation, but if we continue to behave like a Great Power we shall soon cease to be a great nation.' These were pertinent words. Britain was dwarfed by the 'superpowers' after 1945; it was a donkey alongside a bear and a buffalo. It was, however, very clearly the third most powerful nation on earth, and the psychological readjustment of the British imperial psyche could not happen overnight. Britons were still just congratulating themselves on winning the war; they could hardly be expected to detach themselves from world affairs quickly or totally. Foreign policy reflexes would first have to be deconditioned by experience. Even so, as we shall see, Labour did cut down British commitments – in Greece, India and Palestine – and saw the need to draw the United States into sharing the burdens of European defence.

But how consistently did Labour try to solve foreign policy issues without resort to force? Could Bevin have secured agreement with the Soviet Union, or was he initially prejudiced against the communists, perhaps from his earlier tussles within the trade union movement? At times, his language to the Soviets was less than diplomatic. It was a mistake to tell Molotov in October 1945 that he resembled Hitler. Nor was it wise to complain that the Soviet Union was putting its neck out too far and that one day it would be chopped off. In fact the Soviets found it all too easy to make Bevin lose his temper. Nevertheless, it seems certain that although his language was sometimes inept, at first he hoped to reach agreement with both the USA and the USSR. It was an uphill, perhaps a hopeless, struggle. The 'grand alliance' of 1941–5 had never been harmonious, the only bond between the Anglo-American and Soviet 'partners' being their hatred of the common German enemy. The imminence of German defeat had brought friction to the surface at Yalta in February 1945 and by the time of the Potsdam conference in July and August relations between the former allies were distinctly frosty. Stalin's failure to honour the Yalta agreements, by holding free elections in Poland and elsewhere, may have stemmed primarily from defensive concerns, but it gave the West reason to be fearful; and after the failure of appeasement in the 1930s, it is quite understandable that British politicians saw the need to stand firm. Feeding on mutual suspicions, the Cold War gathered a momentum of its own. Moreover, though Bevin may have made mistakes, the Soviets surely made more. Stalin and Molotov could have reached amicable compromises with the British, if they had wanted to. They certainly had reliable knowledge of British intentions through their spies Burgess and Maclean. By 1947 Bevin admitted defeat and fell back on his alternative policy, partnership with the USA and western Europe.

The next pertinent question is whether, out of fear of Soviet aggression, Britain sacrificed its independence of action and so became less an ally than a satellite of the USA. The initial American loan and then the Marshall Plan make it seem as though the USA had purchased British complicity. A good prima facie case can certainly be made out for this. The USA seemed to drag Britain into a war, in Korea in 1950, that was of no direct concern to it, and at a very high cost in terms of expenditure, unpopularity and Cabinet disunity. In addition Britain, as early as the summer of 1946, agreed that in an emergency the USA could send B-29 bombers from five British bases on atomic-bomb raids. By mid-1950, before the Korean war, the US Air Force had eight airfields in Britain, and the Labour government had little effective control over the American atomic weapons on its soil. No wonder Orwell depicted Britain in *Nineteen*

Eighty-Four as 'Airstrip One', merely a province of the super-power 'Oceania'.

Nevertheless, this interpretation is inadequate for several reasons. It was Britain and not the USA which first decided that there could be no agreement with the Soviet Union. It took longer for the Americans to realise that the wartime alliance was over. British politicians and officials certainly had no sense of intellectual inferiority to the Americans, whatever the im-balance of economic and military power between the two countries. They would play Greece to the new Rome. The Truman doctrine, of March 1947, in which the USA agreed to 'support free peoples who are resisting attempted subjugation' – a landmark in the origins of the Cold War – was precipitated by Britain's unilateral decision to withdraw support from Greece and Turkey. America was not forcing Britain to take up foreign policy positions, and on key issues Britain was immune to US advice. Certainly the development of a British atomic bomb was contrary to American wishes and indeed was undertaken because the British were not yet certain of US support in Europe. It also betokened considerable anger that the Americans were reneging on wartime agreements to share the nuclear technology which they had first developed in conjunction with the British. In addition, if the Americans had had their way, British policy would have been different in Palestine; and Bevin, whose insults were not confined to the eastern bloc, went so far as to complain that US policy was motivated by a desire not to have 'too many Jews in New York'. Had Britain been the marionette to the American puppeteers, its policy on European unity would also have been different and it would not have recognised Mao's Communist China in October 1949, over twenty years before the USA did so. Small wonder Attlee once said that Bevin's greatest achievement was 'standing up to the Americans'.

The North Atlantic Treaty Organisation, set up in April 1949, was a landmark in British foreign policy. Its members, including the USA, Canada, Britain and nine European nations, agreed to regard an attack on any one of them as an attack on them all and to take action accordingly. It was the sort of alliance which might well have prevented the First and Second World Wars, while many historians have judged that it may well have prevented a third. Britain had traditionally avoided such an entangling alliance, but it was not forced by the USA on a reluctant Britain. Indeed, it signalled an even greater revolution in US policy than in British. On the contrary, Bevin and Attlee supplied not only the political will for NATO but many of its ideas as well.

Britain was in many ways dependent on the Unites States after 1945. Labour politicians knew this. They recognised that they needed American financial aid to prevent bankruptcy and military support to ensure their own defence and that of western Europe. Yet they were also determined to have an unfettered world role of their own. They would enjoy American support to an unprecedented degree but would use this partly to ensure that they could pursue policies independent of their ally. They needed to forge a very 'special relationship' indeed! In fact the power of the dollar undoubtedly helped to create a climate of opinion in which Britain was more sympathetic than it otherwise would have been to US foreign policy aims. Here was a situation in which partnership – and certainly not a partnership of equals – could slip imperceptibly into client status and dependency. (Was the line crossed during the Korean war? Or was Britain's relatively low-key military support in the war a skilful attempt to cement the NATO alliance in its early, vulnerable years?) On balance, it does seem that, under the Labour governments, Britain was more an ally than a satellite of the Americans, though for how long this could continue was another matter.

The Commonwealth and Empire

Britain was vitally concerned with the defence of western Europe, but on the issue of closer political and economic union between the nations of western Europe it showed itself at best lukewarm. Attlee had said in 1939 that Europe must federate or perish; but after 1945 his government largely stood aloof from the European movement. In 1951 Britain decided not to join the European Coal and Steel Community (fashioned as 'the first concrete foundations of the European Federation'), a refusal later described by Dean Acheson, the American Secretary of State, as 'the great mistake of the postwar period'. In Bevin's words, Britain would not be 'just another European country'. Of far more concern to Labour was the British Empire and Commonwealth. Indeed, several key Labour figures regarded

Europe and the Commonwealth as alternative foci for British energy. In this situation, the case for Europe tended to go by default.

In imperial affairs, Attlee was determined, above all, that India should be allowed its independence and that the Commonwealth should become a genuinely multiracial body. For decades Labour politicians had been calling for Britain to recognise India's right to decide its own destiny, and yet successive governments had stubbornly conceded too little too late. Now, at the end of the war, Britain's capacity to rule India was ebbing – at least without a massive deployment of troops which, financially and psychologically, seemed out of the question, though how the Conservatives under that old imperialist Winston Churchill would have reacted is very much an open question. The government announced its intentions to withdraw, but Indian politicians had little faith any longer in the word of British politicians. Attlee's first job therefore was to convince them that now, at long last, Britain was about to transfer power. It was a difficult task. His second was to devise some means of leaving, and this proved almost impossible. Simply to pull out of the sub-continent might lead to anarchy: there would be no legacy of goodwill, or favourable international publicity, in that. Power had, if at all possible, to devolve in an orderly way upon recognised political structures, and ones friendly to Britain. But was this possible? Conferences, delegations and missions could not engineer agreement between competing Indian parties, and especially between the Indian National Congress led by Nehru and the Muslim League led by Jinnah, the former wanting above all a united India and the latter calling for the creation of a separate Muslim state of Pakistan. Here was a division that might have led the British to try to rule for a little longer. But instead Attlee took what in retrospect is generally considered a brave decision, but which at the time was a risky gamble. In February 1947 he appointed a new Viceroy, Lord Mountbatten, with the specific brief to withdraw from India by June 1948.

Amid escalating communal tensions and violence, Mountbatten brought forward the date of withdrawal to August 1947, by which date agreements had been hastily secured. India became independent and so too did Pakistan, despite the fact that it occupied two groups of provinces – present-day Pakistan and Bangladesh – separated by a thousand miles of Indian territory. The Labour government succeeded remarkably well in transferring power in a seemingly orderly and dignified manner. The president of India's new parliament called independence 'the consummation of the democratic ideals of the British race', an interpretation devoutly to be wished by the British. Withdrawal could now be interpreted as victory rather than defeat, though diehards in Britain still complained and the word 'scuttle' came almost automatically to Churchill's lips. Moreover both India and Pakistan agreed to join the Commonwealth and so maintained trade and cultural links with Britain. Yet amid the dignity and the ceremony there was bloody communal slaughter resulting in hundreds of thousands of deaths, while millions of refugees left their homes and struggled to cross the newly constructed political borders. Some have argued that a slower withdrawal might have resulted in less confusion and fewer deaths. There will never be any certainty about this; but we should at least recognise that the transfer of power in India was not the glorious achievement it may at first sight appear.

In 1948 Ceylon and Burma followed the new pattern that had now been set, though Burma declined to join the Commonwealth. Palestine was far more difficult. Problems in Palestine, a British mandate since 1919, were in many ways similar to those in India. Here too there were acute communal tensions, in this case involving Arabs and Jews. Here too Britain gave a date for withdrawal and then brought it forward; but in this case there was no political agreement to tie up the ends of empire in orderly fashion. Nor was there any legacy of goodwill, only international obloquy. Problems were complicated by pressure from the United States for Britain to allow extensive Jewish immigration and honour its pledge of 1917 to create a national homeland for the Jews, and by pressure from oil-rich Arab states to safeguard the rights of the indigenous Arab population. A backbench critic accused the government in 1947 of 'two years of planless, gutless and witless behaviour'. Others accused Ernest Bevin of anti-semitism; and Kenneth Morgan believes he was 'emotionally prejudiced against the Jews'.

In fact the situation in Palestine was immensely complicated, so much so that it is hard to avoid the conclusion that no solution to its problems existed. Ideally Bevin wanted compromise, to create autonomous provinces for Jews and Arabs, each controlling its own immigration policy, thereby avoiding partition; but debates in cabinet, in Parliament, in the United Nations and elsewhere revealed that no agreement was possible. With no political solution available, Britain had the unenviable and expensive task of barring entry to the Holocaust survivors and of trying to maintain law and order amidst escalating violence, seen most spectacularly in the blowing up of the King David Hotel in Jerusalem in July 1946. Between the end of the war and the end of the mandate 338 British lives were lost in Palestine. In the words of one of the men on the spot, Britain was 'the ham in the sandwich – we had immense pressure brought to bear on us from both sides'. Perhaps it is not surprising, therefore, that in September 1947 the government decided to cut its losses and hand over responsibility to the United Nations, which then recommended partition. The Arabs refused to accept the UN plan and the British refused the thankless task of trying to implement it. Instead Britain simply abdicated. The High Commissioner left on 14 May 1948, as the new state of Israel was proclaimed. Civil war would determine the political geography of the region.

When, a little after this, his wife asked him to unravel a tangled ball of wool, Attlee accepted with alacrity, musing that it was refreshing to find a problem that actually had a solution. This reaction was understandable after Palestine, and so was his horror when it was mooted that Britain might accept as new mandates colonies taken away from Italy. In fact Attlee had little genuine interest in the existing colonies, and he consistently underrated his unflamboyant but dedicated and constructive Colonial Secretary, Arthur Creech Jones. Nevertheless, his government has much to its credit in its colonial activities. Creech Jones forged a policy of devolving greater measures of self-government on the African colonies, while at the same time fostering economic, social and educational improvements. Wishing to avoid the mistakes made in India before 1945, Britain followed a policy, at least in West Africa, of 'nation building'. Colonial governments were to work with the elite of educated West Africans and not indulge in sterile repression. The achievement of independence in Ghana (formerly the Gold Coast) in 1957 and in Nigeria in 1960 owed much to the postwar Labour governments. When the Conservatives were elected in 1951 they were unable to stem the pace of rapid decolonisation. Progress was slower elsewhere in Africa because of the complicating factor of white settlers, and indeed in Central Africa Labour planned a settler-dominated federation, as a lesser evil than the spread of South African apartheid to the north. In Malaya the Labour government authorised the use of British forces to combat Communist guerrillas from 1948.

Overall, Labour's contribution to the end of the British Empire was profound. By 1951 only 70 million people outside the United Kingdom were ruled by Britain, compared with 457 million in 1945. Not only was the all-white Commonwealth club breached in 1947, when India and Pakistan opted to join, but further members were being groomed for admission. Malaya entered in 1957, despite the continuance of guerilla warfare. Equally important, the rules for Commonwealth admission were changed. Hitherto, all member states had accepted the British monarch as their head of state. But in 1949 it was formally recognised that republics could enter. The London declaration of April 1949, which owed much to the Under Secretary of State at the Commonwealth Relations Office, Patrick Gordon Walker, defined the Crown as merely the 'symbol' and the Monarch as 'head' of the Commonwealth. This shrewd form of words enabled Labour's new multiracial Commonwealth to survive: diversity triumphed over uniformity, though at the expense of cohesion, so that Commonwealth 'unity' was not to preclude actual warfare between member states. While to some this Commonwealth has been an invaluable experiment in inter-racial co-operation between individuals as well as governments, to others it has been a dangerous delusion, perpetuating the myth of British power and prestige in the world and detracting attention from more realistic roles. Perhaps it has been both.

7

Conclusion: the Labour governments in perspective

What conclusions may be reached about Attlee's governments? First, what verdict did contemporaries give? The electorate had opportunities to judge Labour's administration in the general elections of 1950 and 1951. In the first Labour won a small overall majority. In the second it gained slightly more votes than the Conservatives but fewer seats and so left office. These results were certainly not the wholehearted endorsement which Labour had wished to see. On the other hand, we may be surprised that its vote held up so well, given that the period after 1945 saw not only popular reforms but also an unpopular intensification (to Crippsian levels) of the austerity which had first begun in wartime. In the adverse economic situation after the war, when it was necessary to borrow massive amounts of money merely to stave off bankruptcy, any government was likely to become unpopular with electors demanding higher standards of living as compensation for the privations of war.

These election results seem even more substantial because, in 1950 and 1951, Labour was challenged by a more effective Conservative party. Lord Woolton had improved the Tories' organisation, so that by 1950 they had twice as many full-time agents as Labour; and R.A. Butler had helped to modernise their policy, bringing about an acceptance of the welfare state and a managed economy. The Conservatives accepted Labour's recent reforms but also promised to 'set the people free' from petty

71

government regulations, an attractive combination of commitments. In addition, Labour had, in its Representation of the People Act of 1949, redrawn constituency boundaries to its own disadvantage: it now tended to enjoy a large number of huge majorities in safe constituencies.

One should not, however, assume that votes cast in 1950–1 were a well-considered verdict on British history since 1945. Often voters are influenced by immediate issues, and this was particularly so in 1951. Labour's defeat in this year was in many ways a reflection on the short-lived 1950–1 government, which suffered setbacks without countervailing successes. Participation in the Korean war necessitated unpopular policies, including an extension of conscription from eighteen months to two years and social services cuts that led to the resignations of Bevan and Wilson. Moreover, the new international economic climate intensified British rationing at a time when France and West Germany seemed to be faring much better. Labour's front-bench team was also weakened by the deaths of Bevin and Cripps; and Herbert Morrison was widely seen as a failure as Foreign Secretary. He had the bad luck to hold this office at a time when the Iranians decided to nationalise the Anglo-Iranian Oil Company, including the world's largest oil refinery at Abadan, without securing the agreement of the British owners. Morrison argued for military action – and the First Sea Lord insisted that the public was 'tired of being pushed around by Persian pipsqueaks' – but the cabinet as a whole was cautious. Although we are likely today to compare favourably Labour's reaction to this crisis with that of the Conservatives in the Suez fiasco of 1956, Morrison was widely criticised in the press.

Labour's strength in the 1951 election may seem remarkable in view of these immediate problems. Indeed, it can be argued that, given just a little luck, the party might well have gone on to form a third administration. Had the government been able to hold on for a little longer, until trade and the economy improved, it might well have secured a majority. Had the Liberals not fielded far fewer candidates than in 1950 (109 compared to 475), the Conservatives might not have won.

Yet it is a common argument that, although Labour might easily have been victorious, its creativity was exhausted by 1951. Admittedly, Labour's leading figures were old and tired – or dead – by 1951, but was the party, in John Saville's words,

'morally and politically bankrupt'? In his view 'Labour socialism had arrived at a dead end.' Certainly in opposition Labour
split into the 'Gaitskellites' and the 'Bevanites', two factions
that seemed for the rest of the decade far more concerned to
attack each other than to harry Conservative ministers. Yet the
disciplines of office might well have produced other results, and
there was still a good deal of talent in Labour ranks. We should
never be too cocksure about 'what might have happened'.

By 1951 Labour was a consolidationist party, or at least its
leading figures were. In the 1951 manifesto the party did not call
itself 'socialist' at all, and there were some who wished to drop
the commitment to nationalisation completely. Had Labour's
political position therefore been clarified by 1951? Are we
finally able to discern the true nature of its 'socialism'? Probably
not. The party's position at the election provided merely a
snapshot within a moving and extremely varied picture. The
consolidationists were for the moment in control, seeing Labour
as a party of social reform or social democracy, but there were
powerful voices in favour of democratic socialism in the wings.
The debate was not yet complete. What was clear was that by
1951 Labour was identified more than ever before with social
welfare reforms and that these gave the party a distinctive voice.
But, even so, the electorate could be forgiven in 1951 for being
somewhat confused. Voters were given a choice between a
Labour party which, to its socialist critics, was tending towards
conservatism and a Conservative party which, to its right wing,
had under Butler's influence committed itself to basically socialist policies.

In 1951 there did seem to be a broad political consensus, later
described as 'Butskellism'. Elements of this consensus had
existed ever since 1940: in the face of the Nazi threat British
politicians had been bound to forget some of their partisan
differences – some but by no means all. 'Consensus' is a relative
not an absolute term; nor does it denote a static reality.
Consensus had developed during 1940–51, a period during
which Attlee and his ministers had pushed the middle ground in
British politics leftwards by their policies. When the Conservatives returned to power in 1951 they accepted many of the
reforms they had criticised whilst in opposition. Their only
major alterations were to introduce prescription and other NHS
charges and to privatise steel and road haulage. But this was not

complete consensus, and indeed some historians doubt whether the term is apt for the true state of politics around 1951. The issue is hotly debated.

The period 1945–51 is therefore one that is closely connected with 1940–5 but also with the years from 1951 onwards. Nowadays 1940–51 is often taken as a period of study; but it is scarcely a homogeneous one, and, despite the change of government, there was no sharp break in 1951. Perhaps 1945–78 should be lumped together, as what Morgan calls the 'Age of Attlee'? Both periodisations, perhaps, have their justification and their uses (as would others). Must we prefer one to the other? A philosopher once wisely remarked that there are in history no beginnings and no ends.

How should historians characterise Attlee's reforms? Many have judged that their acceptance by the Conservatives shows their essentially moderate nature. Might it not also show their constructive character? Attlee often said that he aimed to produce reforms that would last and survive a Tory election victory. Much given to cricketing analogies, he always expected that sooner or later the other side would have their turn to bat. For that reason, he insisted, Labour should proceed empirically and not be afraid of partial solutions. He aimed realistically to bring about a better society, not a perfect one. It was certainly this seemingly mild and unimpressive man who set the tone for the government. Instead of calling him a 'poor man's Baldwin', it may be more apt to consider Baldwin a 'poor man's Attlee'. Rivals thought that they had far more ability and deserved to replace him as premier, but their efforts came nowhere near to success. Instead of accepting Churchill's jibe that he was a modest man with plenty to be modest about, many will be tempted to agree with Morgan that, beneath his diffidence, Attlee was really an 'immodest man with plenty to be immodest about'.

Attlee's Labour governments gave the lie to the prophets of doom. 'Socialism' in the abusive sense of Churchill and others did not come about. No political police clamped a clumsy hand over the mouth and nostrils of the average British citizen. Civil liberties were not taken away. There was an increase in bureaucracy, and sometimes prosecutions were made for petty reasons – a costermonger with a licence to sell vegetables was prosecuted for daring to sell rhubarb, which was classified as fruit; a farmer was prosecuted for slaughtering pigs on the wrong day, another for doing so in the wrong building. Amidst coupons, restrictions, allocations, licences and permits, the 'spiv' flourished, as he had during the war. But bureaucratic excesses were an irritation rather than a serious attempt to stifle political liberty. From the standpoint of 1951, Churchill's Gestapo speech seemed even more irrelevant than it had in 1945. Britain had assuredly not, despite Hayek's views, fought foreign tyranny only 'in order to lose our Liberties to the Bureaucrats at Home'. Political liberties were intact, and by the end of Labour's period in office valuable social and economic liberties had been added. Indeed, by 1951 they were perhaps even taken for granted. That is a measure of Labour's success.

If the fears of 1945 were given the lie, what of the hopes expressed at the election? A good case can be made that they were realised. After all, Labour largely fulfilled its manifesto commitments. The keystone of the welfare state, a National Health Service, was built, buttressed by the National Insurance and National Assistance Acts and the implementation of family allowances. In addition, there was a host of other, more minor but still beneficial reforms – especially in the social and legal fields – that are easily overlooked. Furthermore, 10 per cent of British industry was nationalised. Labour is surely to be praised for managing to implement its pledges so fully, despite an adverse economic and financial climate. If as our criteria to measure Labour's achievement we take into account (a) its aims and whether it achieved them, and (b) the circumstances of the time and the constraints on government action, then the Labour governments have much to their credit. According to Hennessy, Attlee presided over this century's 'most hyper-achieving peacetime administration'. Labour also scores highly when we compare its work with that of other British governments this century. Only the prewar Liberal government of Asquith has a record of social reform that is in any way comparable. It is also arguable that a Conservative government elected in 1945 would have acted very differently from Labour, perhaps allowing economic circumstances to stifle reform, almost certainly interpreting differently wartime plans that rarely amounted to blueprints.

But what did Labour's reforms really amount to? Was there, in any sense, a revolution in these years? Attlee referred to 'revolution without tears' and a 'peaceful revolution'. Roy Hattersley has called him the 'reasonable revolutionary'. Such verdicts may be dismissed as self-interested; but historians of the repute of Ben Pimlott and Trevor Burridge have used the term 'social revolution' about these years. Certainly revolutionary changes did come about in the lives of those who gained most from the new dispensation, as shown by 'oral history' studies of the impact of the NHS. We do well to respect such personal testimony.

Nevertheless, it has seemed to many historians that a better case can be made for the unrevolutionary nature of the changes wrought by Attlee's governments. John Strachey had been a revolutionary before 1945; but as a minister after 1945 he described himself as a 'staid old middle of the road reformist'. Indeed, in its 1950 election manifesto the party claimed only that 'by and large the first majority Labour Government has served the country well'. Certainly the governments were institutionally conservative. Apart from abolishing the anomalies of University seats in the House of Commons and the additional business vote (for those who owned businesses outside their constituency of residence), they made only one change to the British constitution – restricting the delaying power of the House of Lords to two sessions – and this introduced no real change of principle. Indeed even this minor reform came about, in a sense, by accident, by the mistaken belief that it was needed to get the Steel Bill onto the statute book. The monarchy experienced no significant change, and the civil service underwent a return to traditional ways, as businessmen and academics recruited during the war returned to their former occupations. As for that other bastion of the establishment, the public school system, it flourished as never before. Under the stimulus of Eleven Plus failure, many parents for the first time sent their children to independent schools.

A carefully balanced judgement has to be made, recognising the beneficial impact of much-needed reforms and yet admitting that the new system had several inadequacies. We should not underrate the impact of Labour's reforms, but on the other hand it is clear that several of their achievements – like a comprehensive national health service and the raising of the school-leaving age – had been aims of progressives since 1918 and had been high on the political agenda for several years before 1945. Perhaps Labour was remedying the evils of the past rather than setting a challenging agenda for the future. Nor did Labour's measures seem greater than the sum of their parts: indeed, to many, the whole seemed strangely less than its components.

Anthony Howard judged that Labour's election in 1945 brought about 'the greatest restoration of traditional social values' since the Restoration of Charles II in 1660. This is surely an exaggeration, but Attlee's governments were nevertheless disappointing even to many Labour supporters. By 1951 there was an unmistakable unease among many on the left. Even before election defeat, nationalisation had become unpopular with some and was considered irrelevant by others. Public ownership, the party's most distinctive policy, was not the abject failure some right-wing thinkers would have us believe, but neither had it proved a spectacular success or brought about revolutionary changes in the economy or industrial relations. The welfare state was much more popular, and we should be sceptical of the thesis that by costing too much it handicapped British industry from competing effectively with its rivals. Even so, it has become clear that the welfare state – while advantageous in many ways – did not eliminate (though it much reduced) poverty. Nor did it alter the class nature of British society. The fact that benefits were universal proved a boon to many middle-class and wealthy Britons, who were not only more adept at claiming their rights than the poor but saved on private insurance. In short, the welfare state brought about no real redistribution of wealth in British society. Dalton, describing inheritance as 'a fatty degeneration of property', may have raised death duties, but at the same time he increased the exemption limit. There was certainly no significant redistribution of wealth in 1945–51. Available figures indicate no more than marginal changes. One per cent of the population owned 50 per cent of the country's private capital around 1950.

Few would disagree that Attlee's governments were reformist or that they achieved much. Morgan argues that they were among the most effective of all British governments since 1832, bringing the 'Labour movement to the zenith of its achievement as a political instrument for humanitarian reform'. But was there not too much continuity with the past for the adjective 'revolutionary' to be suitable? And should the term 'socialist' be used of Attlee's reforms? Anthony Crosland argued in the 1950s that the old capitalist system no longer existed after 1951. But if this was so, then surely it was primarily a new capitalist system, rather than socialism, that had taken its place. In the 'mixed economy' the public sector was the 'light cavalry', to use the phrase Bevan hoped would more aptly describe the private sector, or maybe merely the ambulance wagon. Attlee and his ministers may have intervened far more in the economy than any previous peacetime government, but they systematically removed the physical controls over the economy first established during the war and began to rely much more on Keynesian 'demand management'. There was nothing specifically 'socialist' about this. Certainly Labour did not, as promised in its 1945 manifesto, 'plan from the ground up' in its 'national plan'. Britain achieved socialism under Attlee only in the weakest sense of that word, as a less acutely class-dominated society with greater equality of opportunity. If all were equal, assuredly some were still more equal than others.

The construction of around a million new council houses after the war, together with the inauguration of the NHS, were hardly examples of private enterprise. Yet Bevan was wrong when he insisted that public enterprise would prove its superiority to the private sector. The middle classes have not flocked to occupy better-built council houses; nor has private medicine disappeared. On the other hand, we should not gainsay the real benefits that came to millions of people from the NHS and council houses of a good standard. Once again, we come back to the fine line that has to be drawn in any critical assessment of the Attlee governments.

Those who, as their major criterion in judging Labour, compare its achievements with some theoretical model of socialism, may well conclude that Attlee's governments should be censured rather than praised. Similarly harsh judgements may be made by those who focus on the opportunities for reform which were missed from 1945 to 1951. Yet such people are all too apt to forget the beneficial changes that were brought about, as well as the hostile environment in which the governments had to operate. At the opposite end of the spectrum, other, more utilitarian, judges may conclude that despite adverse conditions Attlee's ministers did more good to more people than any other government this century, leaving

Britain a better place for their efforts. But amidst such praise there is often no recognition of the governments' failures, blind spots and inadequacies.

Judging these governments is no easy task. By concentrating on what was not done or on what should have been done, harsh verdicts tend to ignore the real improvements which were achieved and which seem all the more significant when set against a background of intractable economic realities. Favourable verdicts, however, while seeing the period from the perspective of the policy-makers themselves and explaining their decisions and actions on the basis of documented evidence, sometimes make the past seem inevitable, as though the decisions taken were the only ones possible. The result is sometimes to gloss over mistakes, as well as the disappointments felt so acutely by many contemporaries. But there are other difficulties too in judging Attlee's governments. Discussion in this chapter has focused on domestic achievements, but some would say that Labour's foreign policy is more basic to any assessment. Compared to the origins of the Cold War and the formation of NATO, issues like council housing and national insurance may seem decidedly parochial. Or perhaps the achievement of Indian independence is more fundamental – certainly it affected the lives of hundreds of millions of people – or the abrupt ending of the Palestinian mandate, which has proved so fateful for the subsequent history of the Middle East. The fact is that there can be no agreed order of precedence for Labour's achievements. At different times historians select different areas of its work for scrutiny, often when contemporary developments make particular aspects seem relevant. E.H. Carr's dictum that history is an 'unending dialogue between the present and the past' is quoted so often because it is true.

British history between 1945 and 1951 is a rich historiographical field. Students are urged to read widely and learn much more about these years than can be confined within such a slim volume as this. But as well as learning about this period – a pleasant and relatively easy undertaking – it is also necessary to reach provisional judgements about the work and worth of the Labour governments. This is an activity which many will find difficult and therefore unpleasant – and, paradoxically, the best students will probably be those least satisfied with their efforts. But it is only by attempting to make such judgements that we come close to an understanding of – as distinct from knowledge about – the past. Hence this book ends without a simple, textbook verdict which may well inhibit each reader's own thinking and which will certainly do less than justice to the complexity of such an important period in British history.

Further reading

Place of publication is London unless otherwise stated.

Attlee's postwar governments have been excellently served by historians, so much so that only a small selection of books can be recommended here. The best surveys are provided by Kenneth Morgan, *Labour in Power, 1945–51* (Clarendon Press, Oxford, 1984), and Henry Pelling, *The Labour Governments 1945–51* (Macmillan, 1984). Morgan's is the longer and fuller account; Pelling's has less analysis but is stronger on narrative. A recent book by Peter Hennessy, *Never Again: Britain 1945–1951* (Cape, 1992), was published after this pamphlet was substantially completed, but it is a wide-ranging, detailed and very significant study, even if somewhat idiosyncratic, and is strongly recommended, as is Hennessy's excellent survey 'The Attlee Governments 1945–51' in Peter Hennessy and Anthony Seldon (eds), *Ruling Performance: British Governments from Attlee to Thatcher* (Blackwell, Oxford 1987).

All the leading figures of the government except Cripps have been well served by biographers. On Attlee there are two notable studies, both sympathetic: Kenneth Harris, *Attlee* (Weidenfeld & Nicolson, 1982), and Trevor Burridge, *Clement Attlee* (Cape, 1985). Bevin is well served by Alan Bullock, *The Life and Times of Ernest Bevin*, vol.3, *Foreign Secretary, 1945–1951* (Heinemann, 1983); Bevan by two highly contrasting works, both of which are indispensable: Michael Foot, *Aneurin Bevan*, vol.2, *1945–1960* (Davis Poynter, 1973), and John Campbell, *Nye Bevan and the Mirage of British Socialism* (Weidenfeld & Nicolson, 1987). B. Donoughue and G.W. Jones, *Herbert Morrison: Portrait of a Politician* (Weidenfeld & Nicolson, 1973), is another weighty and important study. Even weightier is Philip Williams, *Hugh Gaitskell* (Cape, 1979). Ben Pimlott's *Hugh Dalton* (Cape, 1985) is an excellent biography, while Pimlott's edition of *The Political Diary of Hugh Dalton 1918–40, 1945–60* (Cape, 1986) is the most quotable source for this period. Other diaries worth consulting are P. Williams (ed.) *The Diary of Hugh Gaitskell* (Cape, 1983), and Robert Pearce (ed.) *Patrick Gordon Walker: Political Diaries, 1932–71* (Historians' Press, 1991).

The Second World War is essential background for an understanding of 1945–51. Angus Calder, *The People's War* (Cape, 1969), is a standard and very informative work. Paul Addison, *The Road to 1945* (Cape, 1975), should be read alongside Kevin Jeffreys, *The Churchill Coalition and Wartime Politics 1940–45* (Manchester University Press, Manchester 1991). Jeffreys is far less convinced than Addison of the existence of strong consensus during the war. Correlli Barnett, *The Audit of War* (Macmillan, 1986), provides a challenging theory which cannot be ignored.

Among general studies on Labour history the following have stimulating and often highly contrasting accounts of Attlee's years: Keith Laybourn, *The Rise of Labour* (E.J. Arnold, 1988); J. Hinton, *Labour and Socialism* (Wheatsheaf, Brighton, 1983); John Saville, *The Labour Movement in Britain* (Faber, 1988); and David Howell, *British Social Democracy* (Croom Helm, 1976). Peter Clarke, *A Question of Leadership* (Penguin, Harmondsworth, 1990), is a thoughtful collection of essays, several of which are relevant to 1945–51.

On social and economic matters, there are numerous important studies available. Among the most important and accessible are Paul Addison, *Now the War is Over* (Cape, 1985), and Alec Cairncross, *Years of Recovery* (Methuen, 1985). On nationalisation, D.N. Chester, *The Nationalisation of British Industry* (HMSO, 1975), is a seminal work; William Ashworth, *The State in Business* (Macmillan, 1991), is an excellent summary of recent research. M. Sissons and P. French (eds), *Age of Austerity 1945–51* (Penguin, Harmondsworth, 1964), is a wide-ranging and still invaluable collection of essays. For the NHS, Charles Webster, *The Health Services since the War*, vol.1, *The National Health Service before 1957* (HMSO, 1988), is a major work.

Many of the above studies, and in particular Bullock's biography of Bevin, deal with Labour's foreign policy. Space forbids mentioning more than a few specialised and particularly valuable studies. A.S. Milward, *The Reconstruction of Western Europe 1945–1951* (Methuen, 1984), is a challenging reinterpretation. Anne Deighton, *The Impossible Peace: Britain, the Division of Germany, and the Origins of the Cold War* (Clarendon Press, Oxford, 1990), is also important. For the British Empire, see R.J. Moore, *Escape from Empire* (Oxford University Press, Oxford, 1983), on India, and Wm. Roger Louis, *The British Empire in the Middle East 1945–51* (Oxford University Press, Oxford, 1984), on Palestine.

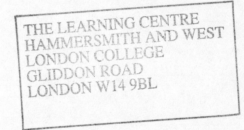